BIRDS of the PACIFIC NORTHWEST for kids

Illustrations by Bologna Sandwich
Photography credits on page 207

Timber Press
Workman Publishing
Hachette Book Group, Inc.
1290 Avenue of the Americas
New York, New York 10104
timberpress.com

Timber Press is an imprint of Workman Publishing, a division of Hachette Book Group, Inc. The Timber Press name and logo are registered trademarks of Hachette Book Group, Inc.

Printed in Shenzhen, China (APO), on responsibly sourced paper

Text design by Bologna Sandwich; layout by Sarah Crumb
Jacket design by Bologna Sandwich

ISBN 978-1-64326-338-0

A catalog record for this book is available from the Library of Congress.

BIRDS of the PACIFIC NORTHWEST for kids

TOM MYERS

TIMBER PRESS
PORTLAND, OREGON

CONTENTS

AN INTRODUCTION

to Birds of the Pacific Northwest

How do birders know birds? An experienced birder sees a bird fly by for a split second and knows it's a Northern Flicker. They hear a bird and immediately identify it as a Red-tailed Hawk. They see a speck high in the sky and recognize it as a Turkey Vulture. They look at a blurry photo of a little brown bird and confidently say that it's a Song Sparrow. How is this possible? Do birders have superpowers?

When I started birding, it did seem like other birders had superpowers. They saw and heard things that I couldn't. Then I started reading field guides. I explored areas with binoculars, a camera, and a smartphone full of bird apps and started paying attention to birds all the time. It turns out that great birders don't have superpowers. They have experience looking for and identifying birds and are more like detectives than superheroes.

One day, while walking with my sister, I pointed out a Northern Harrier hunting in the distance. She turned to look, and then said, "I don't know how you can even see that. It's like you have superpowers!" I explained that birders are like detectives collecting clues. I saw a large bird of prey flying low and slow over the grass, with its wings held up at an angle. And even though it was far away, I could see that it had a white rump patch. I knew the habitat was perfect for harriers, because they hunt rodents in open areas and roost on the ground in tall grass. A few minutes earlier, I had heard a harrier's raspy call from across the field. I didn't need to get a good look to identify it with confidence. Instead, I used clues—where the bird was, what it was doing, its size and shape, its special field marks, and the sounds it made—and I figured out it was a Northern Harrier.

Don't be discouraged if you go birding and aren't sure what birds you're seeing and hearing right away. Keep learning and practicing your detective skills and you'll get better. And this field guide can help you along the way.

What kind of birder will you be?

A birder is anyone who likes birds and enjoys seeing them in the wild, but there are many types of birders. You could watch birds that visit a feeder at your home or go out and watch birds that live in your neighborhood or in a local park. You could stay close to home and get to know the birds in your area, or you could travel to different places to see birds.

You could memorize birds' field marks, research their behaviors, and learn to identify them from far away or after a quick glance. You could learn to identify birds without even seeing them, relying instead on the calls and songs you hear. Or you might not worry too much about identifying every bird and just enjoy seeing and hearing them without needing to name each one.

You could keep a life list that includes all the birds you've ever seen. Or maybe you'll keep many lists—all the birds you've seen in a certain area or over a certain period of time. To keep track of your sightings, you can use a notebook, an app, or a website. You might draw or paint pictures of the birds you see or take photographs, record videos, or capture audio recordings.

You could look for birds on your own, go birding with friends, or join a group of other birders. You could go for a walk and look for birds—or ride in a car, on a bike, or in a kayak or canoe.

Being a birder simply means you care about birds and take the time to notice them. It means you enjoy seeing and hearing them, you like learning about them, and you care about protecting them. How you watch and enjoy birds is up to you, because birding is for everyone!

What's a spark bird?

A spark bird inspires someone to get interested in birds and become a birder. Maybe it's an exotic or flashy bird encountered on a special trip. Sometimes it's a rare or unusual bird that gets people's attention. Or it could be a common backyard bird that, for whatever reason, catches a person's eye!

What birds are included in this book?

This book includes 300 birds to learn about and then go out and find. It includes full profiles of 107 bird species, with detailed information about their markings, diets, habitats, nests, calls, songs, and more. Some of them are included because they're very common, and a new birder is likely to find them right away. Others are included because they're special to the Pacific Northwest and may not be found elsewhere. And a few others represent a group or family of birds that are found in our region.

Quite a few birds can be found in certain parts of the Pacific Northwest and at certain times of year, but they didn't make it into this book. For example, more than 500 species have been seen in Oregon, but only about 300 species are considered common to the state. If you see a bird that's not mentioned in this book, you may be able to find it in a larger field guide, on a bird app, or on a website. Pay attention to the bird's field marks and try to take a picture or record the bird calling or singing—you may have found a rare bird or an unusual visitor. Some birders, especially those hoping to have long life lists, love when a rare or an unusual bird shows up close to home and will race to see it once they learn about it.

Are the birds grouped in a certain way or in a certain order?

The birds included in this book are presented mostly in taxonomic sequence, which is a special way of organizing animals based on how they're related to one another and how they evolved over time. Ornithologists, scientists who study birds, used to assume that similar-looking birds must be related to each other, but that's not always the case.

Scientists are always learning new things about birds. As they research and learn more, they sometimes realize a bird belongs to another group or is related to other birds in a different way than they expected, so the taxonomic sequence is updated. In an older field guide, birds may be presented in a different order. And in the next field guide you buy, the order might be different still.

In this book, birds are grouped together in sections for a variety of reasons. Kingfishers and woodpeckers, for example, are together because even though they have different diets and habits, these species are part of a larger group of birds and are thought to be related. Gamebirds and grebes aren't closely related, but they happen to be next to each other in the taxonomic sequence—and their names just sound good together!

With some exceptions, the names of the birds and the way they're organized in the book are based on the most recent version of the American Ornithological Society (AOS) Checklist of North American Birds, which includes bird species found in North America and Central America.

What are the parts of a bird called?

Some birders use scientific terms to describe the birds they see, while others like to use more common words. It helps to know these scientific words, even if you don't end up using them yourself. For example, the stripe of feathers that go from a bird's beak up over its eye is often called a bird's eyebrow. However, you'll hear some birders use the scientific term, supercilium (super-SILLY-um), for this part of the bird, which is a good word to know and a fun one to say.

Looking at certain parts of a bird can tell you things about how the bird lives. If a bird has long, thin toes, for example, it probably perches on branches. If a bird has webbed feet,

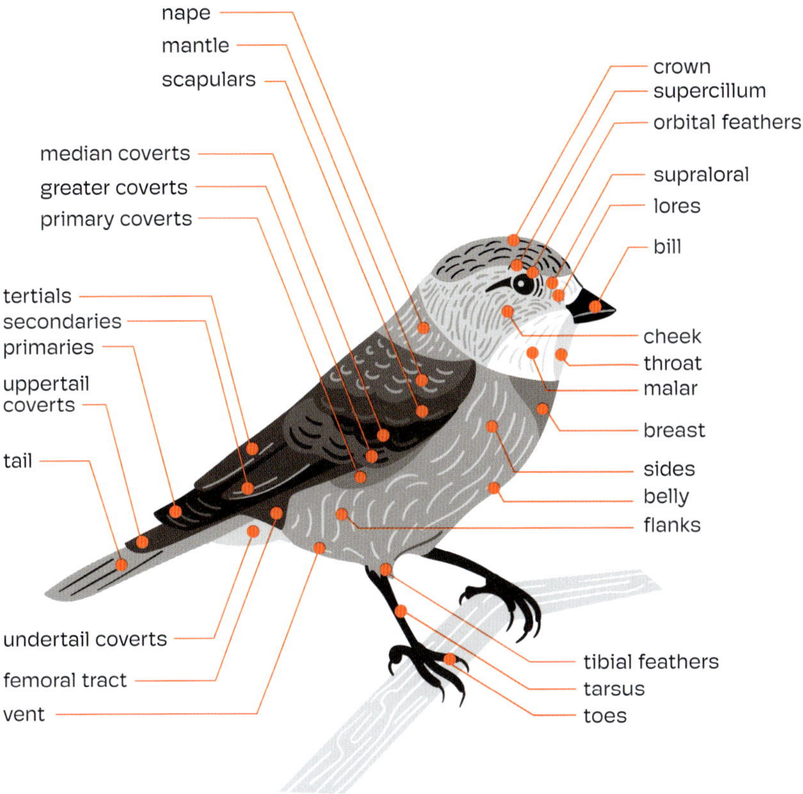

it probably swims. If a bird has thick, sharp talons and a hooked beak, it probably grabs smaller prey and eats meat.

What's the difference between a beak and a bill?

Beak and *bill* refer to the same thing—the two bony protrusions that stick out from a bird's face, where its mouth and nose are located. People tend to use *beak* when they're talking about the pointier ones on songbirds and birds of prey, and they tend to use *bill* when they're talking about the rounder ones on ducks and waterbirds. Ornithologists tend to use *bill* more than *beak*, but both words work.

What is Bird Names for Birds (BNFB)??

You may notice that some birds are named after people, like Steller's Jay or Townsend's Warbler. Many birders think these common names aren't helpful because they don't describe anything about the bird. As a result, the AOS, which assigns the official common names of all birds in North America and Central America, has decided to change the names of birds that are named after people. This will take a few years. When you see the letters *BNFB* next to a bird's common name, it means that the bird was named after a person but will be given a new name soon. BNFB stands for "Bird Names for Birds," a campaign started by a group of birders who think birds should have their own names and not be named after people.

What are the Latin words under each bird's name?

In addition to its common name, each bird has a scientific name made up of two Latin words. The first word is capitalized and is the general name, or genus (JEE-nuhs). Several birds can be included in the same genus. The second name, which is not capitalized, is the bird's specific name, or species (SPEE-sees).

For example, the Barred Owl's scientific name is *Strix varia*. *Strix* is the genus, or general name, for a group of owls that are also called earless owls or wood owls; they're medium-sized to large owls that are mostly nocturnal and don't have ear tufts. The second name, *varia*, is specific to the Barred Owl. The scientific name of its cousin, the Great Gray Owl, is *Strix nebulosa*. You can tell these two owls are related because they're both included in the genus *Strix*, but they're different species.

What are those four letters at the top of some pages?

Scientists use a banding code, a special four-letter code, for each species' common name. It's a short abbreviation they can write in their notes instead of the bird's full name. For birds with a one-word name, like the Bufflehead, the banding code is usually the first four letters (BUFF). For birds with two-word names, like Mourning Dove, the code is usually the first two letters of the first word and the first two letters of the second word (MODO). There are different rules for species with three words in their names and for species with longer or hyphenated names, and there are tons of exceptions to these rules.

Banding codes can be confusing, and people often make mistakes while using them, but some codes are popular among birders and they're good to know about. Some codes are fun to say as words themselves and serve as nicknames for the birds—like MODO for Mourning Dove, LEGO for Lesser Goldfinch, GREG for Great Egret, or TOSO for Townsend's Solitaire!

What do the maps show?

The range maps in this book—or in any book—are meant to show you where a species is most expected and most likely to be seen. Range maps are never exact, and the ranges of some species are ever-changing. Even if the range map of a bird doesn't show a particular location, it doesn't mean you will never see one there. Birds move around at different times of the year and sometimes from year to year.

What do the size symbols mean?

Next to the bird size icons, you'll find letters to indicate its size, like the letters used in clothing labels. The sizes are based on the length of the birds' bodies:

XS	S	M	L	XL
<6"	6–12"	12–24"	24–36"	>36"

Under the size, you'll see the actual length of the bird (the measurement from the tip of its beak to the tip of its tail) and its wingspan (the measurement from the tip of one wing to the tip of the other) in inches.

What's the difference between a song and a call?

Some birds sing—usually to attract a mate or to claim or defend territory. Songs are usually loud, and they can be long and complicated. But birds also communicate using calls, which are shorter sounds. A bird may use calls to warn of a threat or to keep in touch with another bird and share its location.

How do I get started birding?

Remember that most birds are other animals' prey (that is, other animals may eat them), so they're constantly on the lookout for potential danger. This means most birds will see or hear you long before you see or hear them. To see as many birds as possible while you're birding, you should move slowly and quietly. You may have the best luck seeing birds by sitting or standing perfectly still and waiting for the birds to come to you.

Many birders end up hearing more birds than they see. Birds are good at hiding, but they're often singing or making calls. Start listening to birds and learning the songs and calls of the most common birds in your area. In general, try to move slowly and quietly and listen to the sounds around you. Watch for movement and pay attention to the behavior of the birds you see.

Be thoughtful about where and when you go birding. Birds are more active at certain times of day, in certain places, and during certain parts of the year. Depending on what birds you'd like to see, you may want to go early in the morning or at sunset, to a beach or a swamp, during spring migration time or in the middle of winter.

Most birders use binoculars to get a closer look at birds. Some use a scope (also called a spotting scope or telescope) to see birds that are far away. Many birders also use a camera with a zoom, either to take a photo of an unknown bird to try and identify later or simply because they enjoy taking photographs of the birds they see.

All birders make identification mistakes—even experienced ornithologists. When you can't identify a species or you misidentify a species, use it as an opportunity to ask new questions and learn more about birds.

What about backyard bird feeders?

There's nothing like seeing favorite birds visit your own backyard. But to keep those birds healthy you must be sure to clean your feeders and birdbaths regularly and keep the area around them as clean as possible. Many birds can catch diseases from bird feeders and birdbaths that aren't cleaned enough. In fact, sometimes local wildlife agencies ask people to take down their feeders following an outbreak of a contagious disease to prevent it from spreading.

How do birders keep track of the birds they've seen?

Most birders keep a life list of all the species they've seen. Apps and websites, such as the popular eBird, can help you track sightings, including your life list. Some birders keep other lists as well: A year list includes all the species seen during a calendar year (January to December). County lists and state lists include all the species seen in a certain county or state. A yard list includes all the birds a birder has seen at their home. Some birders keep track of birds in very specific lists. A county year list, for example, includes all the species seen in one year in a certain county.

Is there a right way to bird-watch?

Sometimes birders are so excited to get a good look at a bird or to get a clear photograph, that they accidentally flush the bird—they get so close that the bird flies away. Most birders try not to flush birds.

Sometimes birders want to see a species so badly that they'll play a recording, or playback, of the bird's call or song because it might make a bird come closer to investigate a possible mate or rival. Even though it's tempting to do this, most scientists agree that it's not fair to trick a bird in this way. Birds live moment to moment, and a bird that hears your recording and comes to investigate is wasting valuable time and energy that it could be using to find food, build a nest, feed its young, or migrate to another place.

WATERFOWL

Waterfowl, including **geese, swans, and ducks**, have webbed feet and spend time swimming and feeding on or near fresh water. These birds range from the Bufflehead, a duck so tiny that it nests inside old woodpecker holes, to the Trumpeter Swan, a bird that can have a wingspan of up to 10 feet!

SNGO

Snow Goose

Anser caerulescens

FIELD MARKS
- Hefty bill
- White body
- Black wingtips
- Pink legs

HABITAT
Farmed fields, pastures, and wetlands

DIET
Grasses, plants, seeds, and fruits

NEST
Shallow scrape in the ground, lined with feathers

CALLS & SONGS
High-pitched honks

RANGE

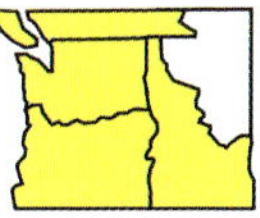

SIZE

Length ~30"
Wingspan ~55"

In winter, flocks of Snow Geese are hard to miss. These mostly white geese blanket the ground in wetlands and fields and can be seen and heard from far away. If you look carefully through a flock, you might spot a goose with a dark body and a white head. Scientists used to think this was a separate species and called it a Blue Goose. But now we know that it's a Snow Goose with different plumage and we call it a blue morph. (*Plumage* refers to a bird's feathers, as a whole.) Plumage can change color according to the season and as a bird ages. Birds lose and replace feathers at various times in their life.

ROSS'S GOOSE

Looks like a miniature version of the Snow Goose with a stubbier bill.

CANG

Canada Goose

Branta canadensis

FIELD MARKS
- Long, black neck
- White cheek and chinstrap
- Black legs and feet

HABITAT
Marshes, lakes, rivers, fields, and parks

DIET
Grasses in warmer months; berries and seeds in colder times

NEST
Big cup of grasses and plants on the ground, lined with feathers

CALLS & SONGS
Low-pitched, nasal honk

RANGE

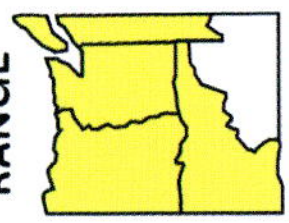

SIZE XL

Length ~25–45"
Wingspan ~45–60"

This familiar goose has a black head and neck, a white cheek and chinstrap, and a brown body. You may hear people mistakenly call this bird a Canadian Goose. They often feed in groups on the ground in grassy areas and fly overhead in a classic V formation. Canada Geese and other waterfowl fly in this shape to help them save energy: as the birds in front flap their wings, the air flowing from their wingtips helps give birds behind them an extra lift. The formation also makes it easier for them to communicate with one another. Canada Geese can be aggressive, especially when protecting nests or young goslings. They'll stretch out their wings and neck, hiss, and even charge at people and their pets if they feel threatened! Several subspecies (which look different or genetically differ from one another) vary in size and color. If you see what looks like a tiny Canada Goose with a short neck and a stubby bill, you might be seeing a Cackling Goose, which is a different species.

CACKLING GOOSE

Looks like a miniature Canada Goose, with a shorter neck and a stubbier bill. It can be as small as a Mallard!

GREATER WHITE-FRONTED GOOSE

Large and grayish brown, with black spots on its belly, earning it the nickname "specklebelly."

BRANT

A medium-sized goose with a black head and neck and a white neck collar. They're usually seen along the coast, but sometimes a Brant will wander inland and join a flock of Cackling Geese.

TUSA

Tundra Swan

Cygnus columbianus

FIELD MARKS
- Black bill
- Black legs
- Yellow spot between eye and bill

HABITAT	DIET	NEST	CALLS & SONGS
Shallow wetlands and flooded fields	Aquatic plants, mollusks, and insects	Huge bowl scraped into a mound of plants	Loud, high-pitched *khoo-oo*

RANGE

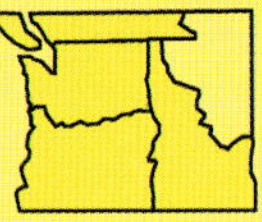

SIZE XL

Length ~52"
Wingspan ~75"

This massive white bird has a long and graceful neck, a black bill, and black legs. When flying, it holds its neck stretched out straight in front. On the water, Tundra Swans feed like dabbling ducks, tipping their bodies forward into the water to root around for food. Tundra Swans and other swans around the world are known for their pair bonds: two swans usually form a pair when they're two or three years old and then feed, roost, and nest together for many years. Visit marshy areas in winter to find these birds. Look and listen closely and you might identify the less common cousin of the Tundra Swan, the Trumpeter Swan.

TRUMPETER SWAN

Looks very similar to the Tundra Swan but with a slightly larger bill. Look closely, and you'll notice that the black of the bill extends up around the eye. It can be hard to tell the difference between these two species, but luckily the Trumpeter Swan makes a clear, trumpet-like honk!

WODU

Wood Duck

Aix sponsa

HABITAT
Woodlands, near standing water

DIET
Aquatic plants, grasses, seeds, berries, and insects

NEST
Tree cavity or nest box

CALLS & SONGS
Males make a high whistle; females call *ooh-eek! ooh-eek!*

RANGE

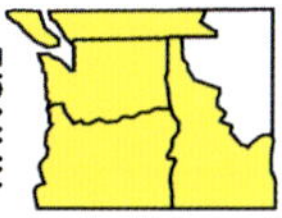

SIZE M

Length ~19"
Wingspan ~30"

Take a walk in a wooded area near standing water and you may see a brightly colored duck perched in a tree, floating at the edge of the water, or flying through the forest. The male Wood Duck has a stunning, colorfully striped crest and bright red eyes, with white stripes on a mix of iridescent (shiny) purples and greens. The female is grayish with a large white patch around each eye and pale spots on her sides. These ducks nest high in tree cavities and can be quite secretive, but if you accidentally get too close to them, they will flush and squeal a loud *ooh-eek! ooh-eek!* as they fly away.

DID YOU KNOW?
Wood Duck ducklings live in nest cavities that can be 50 feet high in a tree. When it's time for the ducklings to leave the nest, they still can't fly and have to jump down! Luckily, at this age, the ducklings can drop very far and land on the soft ground without getting injured.

FIELD MARKS
- Claws for perching in trees
- Droopy crest
- Male: colorful pattern and red eyes
- Female: white patch around eye

FEMALE WOOD DUCK

AMWI

American Wigeon

Mareca americana

FIELD MARKS

- Pale forehead and crown
- Iridescent green eye stripe
- Brownish back

HABITAT
Wetlands, ponds, rivers, and flooded fields

DIET
Aquatic plants and grasses, insects, and invertebrates like snails

NEST
Shallow bowl in the ground, lined with grass and feathers

CALLS & SONGS
Males make high whistle notes; females make husky grunting noises

RANGE

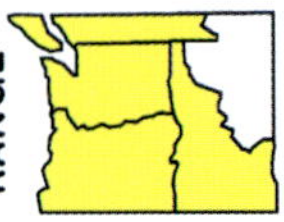

SIZE

Length ~ 20"
Wingspan ~32"

New birders can be overwhelmed by all the different types of ducks. Learn the most common species first, such as Mallards and Wigeons, before learning to identify less common ducks. American Wigeons (WIDGE-uhnz) are best identified by the male's pale forehead and crown (the top of its head) and its iridescent green eye stripe. When you see a pond full of ducks, listen for the high whistles of the American Wigeon over the quacks and calls of other ducks. All birds replace old feathers with new ones by a process called molting. When American Wigeons molt from summer into winter plumage, it takes about 35 days, and during that time, they can't fly!

EURASIAN WIGEON

A cousin from the other side of the world. In the Pacific Northwest, you may see a Eurasian Wigeon mixed in with a flock of American Wigeons, and it will stand out with its reddish head.

MALL

Mallard

Anas platyrhynchos

FIELD MARKS

- Female: brown body, orange-brown bill
- Male: yellow bill, shiny green head, white collar

HABITAT
Lakes, ponds, marshes, and rivers; wet areas in parks

DIET
Aquatic plants and insects, worms, snails, and seeds

NEST
Bowl of plant material on the ground, close to water

CALLS & SONGS
Males make a quiet, scratchy call; females make the classic *quack*

RANGE

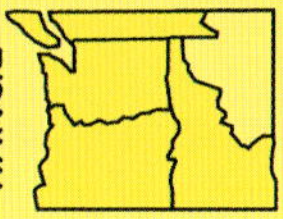

SIZE M

Length ~23"
Wingspan ~34"

If someone were to say, "imagine a duck," you might picture a Mallard in your mind. The male duck, or drake, has a shiny green head, white neck ring, brown chest, and yellow bill. The female, or hen, is streaky brown. She nests on the ground in a soggy spot and will pull down the tall plants growing around her to hide herself and her nest. Male and female Mallards have orange feet and a shiny blue wing patch that's easy to spot when the ducks fly past. As you start to identify more duck species and listen to their calls, you may notice that Mallards are the only ducks that make a true *quack*.

MALE NORTHERN SHOVELER

Has a much larger and wider bill that's shaped like a shovel. Like a Mallard, it has a shiny green head, but it has a a dark bill, white chest and brown flanks (sides).

Other Ducks

Ducks have wide, flat bills that help them filter out food from water and then crush it before eating it. They can be divided into two groups based on how they usually gather food: Dabbling ducks feed at the surface of the water by dabbling—tipping forward to put their heads underwater to feed, with their rear ends up in the air and their feet dangling above the water. Diving ducks dive completely underwater to look for food and are usually found in deeper water. This is one way to describe ducks based on their regular behaviors. Sometimes, a dabbling duck will dive underwater after something or a diving duck might feed at the surface.

Male and female ducks often look quite different from one another. Males are usually flashy and colorful, which helps them attract mates. Females are usually plain and brownish, which helps them blend in with the vegetation where they build their nests. These photos show male ducks.

GADWALL

Grayish brown with a thin, dark bill and black rump patch

NORTHERN PINTAIL

Brown head, white neck stripe, and long, thin tail

CANVASBACK

Large diving duck with a sloped, rust-colored head and white body

REDHEAD

Bright red, rounded head, with a black breast and gray body

LESSER SCAUP

Lesser and Greater Scaups (skops) are diving ducks with dark heads and whitish flanks

RING-NECKED DUCK

Black head, gray flanks, and a white outline around its bill

BLUE-WINGED TEAL

Bluish head with a white crescent in front of each eye

CINNAMON TEAL

Dark red plumage, with a black bill and red eyes

GREEN-WINGED TEAL

Tiny, with a reddish head and shiny green eye stripes

Harlequin Duck

Histrionicus histrionicus

HABITAT
Mountain rivers in summer; near the ocean in winter

DIET
Aquatic inver-tebrates and small fish

NEST
Pile of pine needles, moss, and leaves on a cliff, in a tree, or on the ground

CALLS & SONGS
Squeaks like a mouse

RANGE

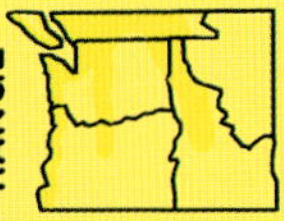

SIZE M

Length ~16"
Wingspan ~25"

The male Harlequin Duck has a unique, colorful look. This tiny sea duck has a dark blue head, reddish flanks, and a complex pattern of white stripes and patches all over. The female is tougher to identify if she's not swimming or standing by a male. She has a messy white patch behind her bill and a clean white spot behind each eye. In winter, Harlequin Ducks are found in rocky areas along the coast, and they often feed in rough waters near sharp rocks. When scientists x-ray these ducks, they often find many broken bones that have healed! This little sea duck spends the breeding season away from the ocean, in the mountains near fast-moving rivers.

FIELD MARKS
- Small bill
- White patches and stripes on face
- White collar
- Reddish flanks

SURF SCOTER

A Surf Scoter (SKOH-ter) has white head patches and a colorful bill that's orange, white, and black. Scoters are sturdy sea ducks that dive for crustaceans and mollusks like clams and mussels.

WHITE-WINGED SCOTER

Has an orange-tipped bill, a white comma-shaped mark near each eye, and a white wing patch.

BLACK SCOTER

Smaller scoter, with a rounded head and a knobby orange bill.

LONG-TAILED DUCK

This is another sea duck to look for at the coast, especially in winter. Male Long-tailed Ducks have an unusual pattern of black, gray, and white patches, and they have superlong tails!

Bufflehead

Bucephala albeola

HABITAT
Marshes, ponds, lakes, rivers, and bays

DIET
Aquatic invertebrates, crustaceans, and mollusks

NEST
Old woodpecker (usually Northern Flicker) holes or in nest boxes

CALLS & SONGS
Usually quiet, but males may chatter and squeal and females sometimes grunt

RANGE

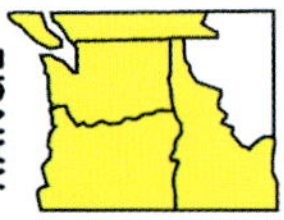

SIZE M

Length ~13"
Wingspan ~21"

This tiny duck is almost always found on water, but nests in old woodpecker holes. It can be spotted easily because of its size and its black-and-white plumage. The male has a white belly and breast, a black back, and a big, round head with a large white patch on the back. In the right light, the feathers on its face are iridescent—they shine in purplish green colors. The female is mostly brownish black with an oval-shaped white patch on its cheek. Usually found in small groups and more likely to be seen in winter, Buffleheads run across the water before taking off, and they fly in a direct path with very fast wingbeats.

FIELD MARKS
- White patch on back of head
- Iridescent face and neck
- Small gray bill
- Black back

DID YOU KNOW?

Goldeneyes are medium-sized sea ducks that are closely related to Buffleheads. They're known for their courtship ritual—the male throws its head backward until it touches its back and then throws it forward and kicks up water with its feet! Male Common Goldeneyes and Barrow's Goldeneyes are easy to distinguish because of the uniquely shaped white patches on their faces, but the females of these two species can be very tough to tell apart.

Has a more peaked crown and a round, white patch in front of each eye.

COMMON GOLDENEYE

(BNFB)

BARROW'S GOLDENEYE

Has a rounder head and a white crescent-shaped patch in front of each eye.

HOME

Hooded Merganser

Lophodytes cucullatus

FIELD MARKS

- Thin, jagged bill
- Yellow eyes
- Male: black-and-white crest
- Female: shaggy brown crest and yellow-brown bill

HABITAT
Ponds, lakes, marshes, and rivers

DIET
Small fish, aquatic insects, crustaceans, mollusks, and more

NEST
Shallow bowl of wood shavings inside a tree cavity, or in a nest box

CALLS & SONGS
Usually quiet, but males make a froglike croak; females grunt *craw-craw-craw*

RANGE

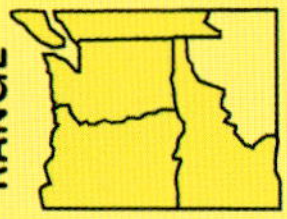

SIZE M

Length ~18"
Wingspan ~24"

The Hooded Merganser (murr-GAN-sir) is a small, secretive duck with a thin, serrated bill. The edge of the bill is jagged like a saw, which helps it grab slippery fish. The male has a large, fan-shaped, black-and-white crest it can raise and lower. The female is grayish brown with a smaller, shaggier, cinnamon-colored crest. When a male does its courtship displays to attract a female, it raises its crest and pulls its head back before dipping forward, snapping its bill shut and letting out a low croak. Like Wood Ducks, these birds nest in tree cavities, and young mergansers leave the nest by leaping down to the forest floor, sometimes from great heights! Mergansers are all fish-eating ducks whose jagged-edged bills give them the nickname "sawbills."

FEMALE HOODED MERGANSER

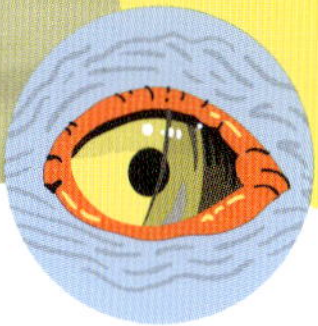

DID YOU KNOW?

All birds have a third eyelid called a nictitating membrane. It's an extra, transparent eyelid that sweeps across each eye side to side (not up and down like a regular eyelid). This membrane keeps their eyes moist and clean and can even protect them from sharp objects. In the case of Hooded Mergansers, the membrane also helps them see underwater, like a pair of swimming goggles, so they can find fish to eat.

COMMON MERGANSERS

Often seen on rivers and larger bodies of water. The male has a round, green head and the female has a shaggy, cinnamon-colored crest.

RED-BREASTED MERGANSER

Usually found on the ocean or nearby, and they have long, very thin bills. The male's crest is shaggy and green and the female's is brownish.

RUDU

Ruddy Duck

Oxyura jamaicensis

FIELD MARKS
- Blue bill
- Stiff tail often raised
- White cheek
- Dark cap

HABITAT
Freshwater marshes, wetlands, and other waterways

DIET
Aquatic insects, crustaceans, and other invertebrates

NEST
Bowl of dried plant material hidden in a woven canopy of vegetation

CALLS & SONGS
Males make burping sounds; females make squeaky whistles

RANGE

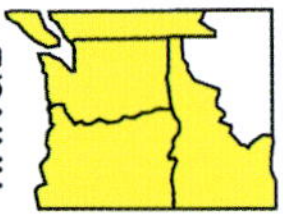

SIZE

Length ~15"
Wingspan ~20"

With a blue bill that curves up like a smile and a stiff tail held up in the air, a Ruddy Duck can look sort of cartoonish. This duck can be fun to watch as it bobs along, diving for food and doing a "bubble display," when a male beats its bill against its inflated neck, making bubbles on the water, and then lets out a low burping sound. These ducks hunt mostly at night. During the day, they often float on the water with their heads tucked back, taking a nap. Since its blue bill and white cheek patch are hidden when it's resting, look for its short, stiff tail, often held up at an angle.

DID YOU KNOW?

Ruddy Ducks lay surprisingly large eggs for such a small duck. Like many ducks, their ducklings are precocial (pre-KO-shull)—they hatch very developed and are active and independent almost immediately. Within a day of hatching, they're swimming and diving for their own food. And after just six weeks, they can fly. Other birds, like many songbirds, are altricial (al-TRISH-ull), meaning they need to be cared for in the nest for two to four weeks before they're independent.

GAMEBIRDS & GREBES

When birders talk about **gamebirds**, they usually mean birds that spend most of their time on the ground (think pheasants). Gamebirds usually feed on seeds or insects and tend to stay hidden in low vegetation. Most of the birds in this group will take flight when flushed, but they fly low to the ground before finding a new place to hide.

Grebes (greebz) are waterbirds with short wings and tails and strange, lobed toes. Their feet are way at the back of their body, making them great swimmers and divers, but not so great at walking.

Gamebirds and Grebes aren't closely related, but they evolved from a common ancestor at around the same time. That's why they appear next to each other in a taxonomic sequence.

CAQU

California Quail

Callipepla californica

FIELD MARKS
- Head plume
- Patterned belly
- Black face outlined in white

HABITAT
Dry grasslands, farming areas, towns, and cities

DIET
Mostly seeds; also invertebrates like caterpillars and snails

NEST
Depression in the ground lined with grass, hidden in thick vegetation

CALLS & SONGS
Three-part call that sounds like *Chi-CA-go* and sharp *wip-wip-wip*

RANGE

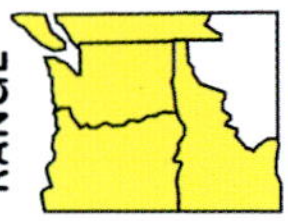

SIZE S

Length ~10"
Wingspan ~14"

These plump gamebirds have stylish, comma-shaped plumes of feathers on their heads and make distinct *chi-CA-go* calls. You may see a group, or covey, of California Quail feeding together or crossing a road. The male has a black face outlined in white and an intricately patterned body with white, brown, and gray dashes. The female is a bit more plain with a smaller head plume. Certain birds will lay eggs in the nests of other birds as well as their own. This behavior is called egg dumping, and lots of ducks are known to do this. California Quail are also egg dumpers, and a single nest can end up with more than 25 eggs!

MOUNTAIN QUAIL

These quail live in smaller coveys in hills and mountainous areas. They have white bars on their brownish sides and thin, straight head plumes.

Other Gamebirds

Many gamebirds in the Pacific Northwest aren't originally from this part of the world. They have been released here on purpose and are popular with hunters as well as birders.

WILD TURKEY

Originally from the eastern half of North America, with shiny plumage, fan-shaped tail, and a featherless head; male makes loud gobbles

RING-NECKED PHEASANT

Originally from Asia, male has an iridescent green head, a red face, and a long, striped tail and makes a loud *koh-kak* call

CHUKAR

Originally from the Middle East and southern Asia, with a white throat outlined in black, a red bill, and dark striped sides; makes a loud *chukar, chukar, chukar* call

GRAY PARTRIDGE

Originally from Europe and Asia, brownish with a reddish face and throat; call sounds like a creaking gate

RUGR

Ruffed Grouse

Bonasa umbellus

FIELD MARKS

- Pointy crest
- Dark tail band
- Barring on belly and flanks

HABITAT
Forests

DIET
Plants and sometimes insects

NEST
Depression on the ground, lined with vegetation

CALLS & SONGS
Usually quiet; squeals or hisses when flushed

RANGE

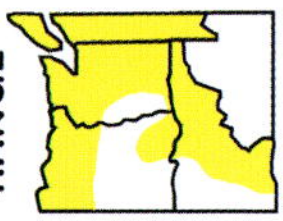

SIZE M

Length ~17"
Wingspan ~21"

These forest birds can be tough to find because they're well camouflaged—in other words, their feather colors blend in with the environment. These chickenlike birds can be reddish, brownish, or grayish. They have pointy crests and fan-shaped tails. Males are known for their courtship displays. The male stands on a log, rock, or stump and raises up its dark neck feathers that form a collar, or ruff—kind of like the frilly collar people used to wear. Once the collar is up, the grouse fans out its tail and starts drumming—beating its wings quickly against its own body, which makes a fast, deep thumping sound that reminds people of a lawn mower starting up! In winter, a Ruffed Grouse will roost by burying itself in the snow. When a skier or snowshoer happens by, the bird bursts out of the snow, and it can be quite a surprise!

DUSKY GROUSE

Much bigger than a Ruffed Grouse. The male has orange-red eyebrows, called eye combs, and a reddish air sac on its neck that inflates during courtship displays.

SOOTY GROUSE

Similar to the Dusky Grouse but usually darker, and its eye combs and air sac are yellow. Both Dusky and Sooty grouse give loud, low hoots.

GREATER SAGE-GROUSE

These grouse don't live in the forest like other grouse. They live in wide-open sagebrush habitat. Males gather in flat, open areas, called leks, where they display their inflated air sacs and make bizarre popping sounds to compete with one another for the attention of females.

PBGR

Pied-billed Grebe

Podilymbus podiceps

FIELD MARKS

- Stubby bill with a black ring in summer
- Almost no tail
- White ring around dark eye

HABITAT
Rivers, ponds, and bays with aquatic vegetation

DIET
Small fish, aquatic insects, and crayfish

NEST
Open bowl on a raft of floating vegetation

CALLS & SONGS
Loud, whooping, gulping, repeating *kow-kow-kow!*

RANGE

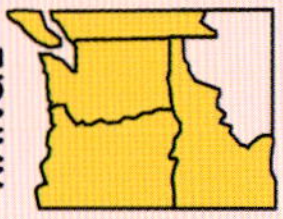

SIZE M

Length ~13"
Wingspan ~21"

This little waterbird can be hard to spot, but once you recognize its loud, wailing calls, you'll often hear it near wetlands or ponds. The Pied-billed Grebe is brownish and has almost no tail. In summer, its thick bill has a dark ring around it. These birds dive underwater for food in an unusual way. They trap air and water in their feathers and can squeeze out the air and sink straight down like a submarine. A nervous Pied-billed Grebe will sink only part way, leaving its head above the water to keep watch. You may spot a family of Pied-billed Grebes in summer, when the black-and-white-striped young, called grebettes, ride on their parents' backs. The grebe's genus name, *Podilymbus*, is Latin for "feet at the back." Like many diving waterbirds, the Pied-billed Grebe's feet are located way at the back of its body. This helps it swim and dive, but takeoffs, landings, and even a short walk on dry land can be pretty awkward.

RED-NECKED GREBE

Larger grebe with a longer neck, a long, thick bill and a reddish or pale neck.

HORNED GREBE (WINTER)

Has a white cheek and a dark cap in winter.

In summer, this grebe has golden feathers, or “horns,” behind its eyes.

HORNED GREBE (SUMMER)

EARED GREBE (SUMMER)

Looks a lot like a Horned Grebe in winter, but with a more peaked head. In summer, they have spiky, golden “ears.”

WEGR

Western Grebe

Aechmophorus occidentalis

FIELD MARKS
- Greenish yellowish bill
- Black cap
- Dark feathers around eye

HABITAT
Breeds in marshes and wetlands; winters on rivers, large lakes, and seaside

DIET
Mostly fish

NEST
Bowl on a mound of floating vegetation

CALLS & SONGS
High, thin *kree-keep*

RANGE

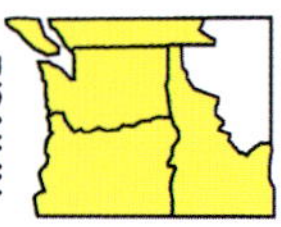

SIZE L

Length ~24"
Wingspan ~36"

These long-necked, black-and-white grebes are known for their incredible spring courtship dances, where two birds run across the surface of the water side by side. In summer, you may see a pair with fluffy chicks riding around on their backs. In winter, they can be seen diving and feeding in groups. Most people are surprised to learn that grebes swallow their own feathers. The feathers form a sort of filter that traps things like sharp fish bones. Otherwise, these objects would damage their digestive systems. Every so often, a grebe spits up a pellet made of feathers, bones, and anything else it can't digest.

CLARKE'S GREBE (BNFB)

Looks almost exactly like its cousin, the Western Grebe. However, a closer look will show that the Clarke's is paler overall, with eyes surrounded by white feathers and a brighter yellowish orange bill.

DOVES, NIGHTJARS, SWIFTS & HUMMING-BIRDS

Doves and pigeons usually have thick, round bodies, with small heads and short legs. They tend to feed on the ground and are fast, strong fliers. **Nightjars** are nocturnal, insect-eating birds that blend in with their perches during the day. **Swifts** may look a bit like swallows, but they have much stiffer wingbeats and are almost never seen perched. Surprisingly, swifts are related to hummingbirds, which are tiny, fast-moving, and colorful birds with long, thin bills. **Hummingbirds** feed mostly on flower nectar and tiny insects.

MODO

Mourning Dove

Zenaida macroura

FIELD MARKS
- Black spots on wing
- Long, pointy tail
- Small, round head

HABITAT	DIET	NEST	CALLS & SONGS
Grasslands, farms, neighborhoods—almost anywhere	Almost entirely seeds	Wobbly pile of twigs, pine needles, and grass	Sad, low *who-WOO, who-who-who*

RANGE

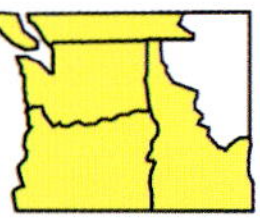

SIZE

Length ~11"
Wingspan ~16"

Many people hear this bird's low *who-WOO, who-who-who* call and think they're hearing an owl. But follow the sound and you'll find a slim, gray-brown dove perched on a branch or telephone wire or on the ground. Get too close and it will make another sound, which can be a surprise to new birders: when it takes off, its wings make a loud whistle. This sound might scare off predators or warn other Mourning Doves that it's time to move on. And these birds can really move! Mourning Doves don't necessarily look fast when they're walking on the ground eating seeds or perched up in a tree, but they can fly faster than 50 miles per hour! Their banding code, MODO, is fun to say, and many birders use it as a nickname for the Mourning Dove. It is one of the most widespread gamebirds in the country, and scientists believe that there are more than 350 million in the United States! They're popular with hunters, and more than 20 million birds are hunted each year.

EURASIAN COLLARED-DOVE

Originally from Europe and Asia. It's larger than a Mourning Dove, with a black patch on its nape (the back of the neck).

BAND-TAILED PIGEON

These huge pigeons are native to the Pacific Northwest and found mostly in forests closer to the coast. They are bluish gray, with a white patch on their nape and a black-tipped, yellow bill.

ROCK PIGEON

Originally from Europe. They can be all white, mostly black, or a mix of colors, but their classic plumage is bluish gray with an iridescent neck and a dark back. When you think of a typical city pigeon, you probably imagine this bird.

CONI

Common Nighthawk

Chordeiles minor

HABITAT
Open areas like fields, clearings in woodlands, and sometimes in towns and cities

DIET
Flying insects

NEST
None

CALLS & SONGS
A buzzy *peent* flight call; males make a booming *whoov!* when they dive

RANGE

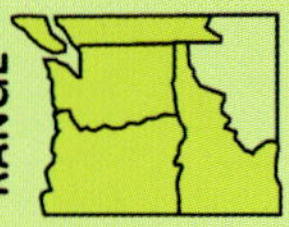

SIZE

Length ~10"
Wingspan ~24"

If you're in the right spot on a warm summer night, you may get a chance to see Common Nighthawks diving and dipping through the air like giant bats, catching flying insects with their huge, gaping mouths. These birds have long, pointed wings and fly with dramatic and graceful swoops. They're most active at dawn and dusk. Nighthawks make a distinct *peent* call while they fly overhead. And males do an incredible dive display to impress females. They dive straight toward the ground and then pull up just before they crash! The sound of the air rushing through their feathers as they change direction makes a bizarre, booming *whoov* sound. During the day, nighthawks can hide in a patch of trees, on the ground, or on a branch because of their speckled feathers that provide camouflage, but sometimes they'll rest on a fence right in the open. They don't even need to build a nest because their eggs and chicks are also well camouflaged.

FIELD MARKS

- Mottled gray-brown feathers
- White bar on wings
- Small bill tip

Common Nighthawk in flight

COMMON POORWILL

Leads a very similar life to its cousin, the Common Nighthawk. But instead of flying around and hunting on the wing, these birds stay perched low to the ground at night and fly up to catch insects that fly past.

VASW

Vaux's Swift (BNFB)

Chaetura vauxi

FIELD MARKS

- Dark, with paler throat
- Long wings
- Short tail

HABITAT
Roosts in old-growth forests or in chimneys

DIET
Insects

NEST
Small twigs held together by saliva, inside a dead tree or in a chimney

CALLS & SONGS
High-pitched, buzzy twitter

RANGE

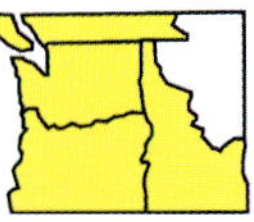

SIZE XS

Length ~5"
Wingspan ~11"

There are places in the Pacific Northwest where birders and nonbirders can spend a fall afternoon or evening watching thousands of tiny Vaux's (VOX-iz) Swifts funnel into an old chimney to roost for the night. These birds spend their days hunting insects on the wing. As they prepare for their southern migration, they gather in huge groups. As the sun begins to set, the swifts swirl around above the entrance to their roost and dive in one by one. It's quite a sight! To add to the entertainment, a predator such as a falcon or hawk will sometimes perch nearby and pass through the tornado of swifts to grab its dinner. Although Vaux's Swifts are famous for the huge groups that roost together in old chimneys, they also roost in smaller numbers around the Pacific Northwest. If you hear a high-pitched twittering coming from a chimney in your home, a few Vaux's Swifts may have decided to roost or nest there.

Vaux's Swifts entering a chimney at dusk

WHITE-THROATED SWIFT

Larger than the Vaux's Swift and spends summers on cliffs in steep river canyons. It has a white throat and white patches on its flanks.

BLACK SWIFT

Very big (for a swift) but hard to find unless you know a nesting site. They spend most of the day feeding high in the sky, and their nests are usually hidden behind waterfalls!

ANHU

FIELD MARKS

- Iridescent gorget and face
- Greenish feathers
- Tiny legs and feet

Anna's Hummingbird

(BNFB)

Calypte anna

HABITAT
Neighborhoods, parks, farmlands, and coastal areas

DIET
Flower nectar, insects, and tree sap

NEST
Tiny cup made of plant material, feathers, and spiderwebs

CALLS & SONGS
High, sharp *chit* calls; male sings scratchy, jumbly, high-pitched squeaks

RANGE

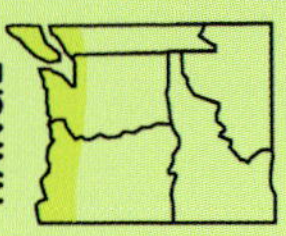

SIZE

Length ~4"
Wingspan ~4.5"

There are several beautiful hummingbird species that visit the Pacific Northwest, but this is the only one that sticks around all year. The male Anna's Hummingbird has a greenish back, a white belly, and a shimmering red throat and head. The patch of throat feathers, called a gorget (GORE-jit), is especially iridescent. In shadow, this hummer can appear dark, but in the sun it flashes bright pink. Females are greenish and can also have some shiny throat feathers. This little bird weighs about the same as a single nickel. Despite their size, they're very territorial and can be aggressive toward one another, particularly around feeders. When a male wants to impress a female, he flies high into the air and then dives down and back up, making a J-shape. At the bottom of his dive, air moving across his spread tail feathers makes a surprisingly loud, sharp *pik!* sound. In winter, especially during cold nights, they conserve energy by going into a hibernation-like state called torpor. Their body temperatures drop, their heart rates slow, and they stay motionless.

RUFOUS HUMMINGBIRD

Orange and greenish, and males have bright orange gorgets.

CALLIOPE HUMMINGBIRD

These hummingbirds are tiny! They're the smallest bird in North America. Males have a streaky purple gorget.

The male Black-chinned Hummingbird has a dark chin and throat.

BLACK-CHINNED HUMMINGBIRD

RAILS, COOTS & CRANES

Rails, coots, and cranes are all related, even though they look quite different from one another. Rails are tiny, secretive birds that stay hidden in dense vegetation and are rarely seen but often heard. Coots look like a cross between a chicken and a duck and are usually found swimming in wetlands. Cranes are huge and have long legs. They travel in noisy flocks and are easy to spot from a distance.

VIRA

Virginia Rail

Rallus limicola

FIELD MARKS

- Long, curved, orangish bill
- Gray face
- Black-and-white-barred (color banded) flanks

HABITAT
Marshes and swamps

DIET
Insects, spiders, snails, crayfish, and small fish

NEST
Basket of woven plant material floating on vegetation or in a cattail clump

CALLS & SONGS
Loud, descending series of grunts and squeaks; song is metallic clicking notes

RANGE

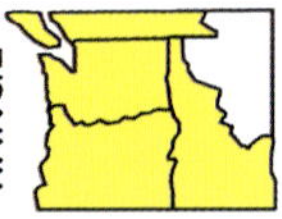

SIZE S

Length ~9"
Wingspan ~13"

These strange-looking, chickenlike marshbirds have long, curved, orangish beaks. They're known to be some of the most secretive birds and are usually hidden in dense vegetation. But once you know their bizarre calls, you'll likely hear them if you visit a marsh. Listen for a loud, descending series of grunts and squeaks. A patient and lucky birder may see this bird step out from a thicket or quickly cross a mudflat. A Virginia Rail may look plump from the side, but when you see one from the front, it's actually very thin! They have what scientists call a laterally compressed body, which helps them sneak between thick vegetation in a marsh.

SORA

Another rail species that is secretive and usually hidden. You may hear this bird in a marsh in spring and summer, and if you're patient and in the right spot, you might even see it. It looks a bit like a tiny chicken, with a short, yellow bill and a short, pointy tail. The Sora's most common calls are a loud and descending whinny and a rising, whistled *koo-wee!*

AMCO

American Coot

Fulica americana

FIELD MARKS
- White bill
- Red eyes
- Lobed toes

HABITAT	DIET	NEST	CALLS & SONGS
Freshwater marshes, lakes, and rivers	Mostly aquatic plants; also insects, small fish, snails, and more	Floating platform made of plant material	Grunts, clucks, croaks, and squawks

RANGE

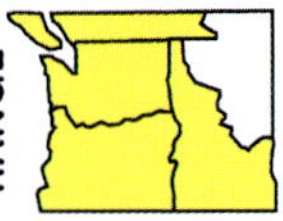

SIZE M

Length ~15"
Wingspan ~24"

Sometimes called mud hens, American Coots do walk and bob their heads like chickens, but they usually act more like ducks. They're dark gray with a white bill and red eyes. Usually seen dabbling or diving in the water, coots will also graze on lawns and mudflats. If you spot one out of the water, you can admire its giant and bizarre-looking lobed toes. The lobes of skin on a coot's toes help it swim in the water but will fold back when it's walking on land. This bird is a strong flier once it's in the air, but it needs a long running start to lift off the water.

DID YOU KNOW?

The American Coot looks like a duck when it's swimming and feeding on a pond. But if you look closely at the shape of its bill and its lobed toes, it's clear that this bird is not a duck at all. In fact, it's much more closely related to the massive Sandhill Crane and the secretive Virginia Rail than it is to any duck. That's why it's included here and not with Mallards and Wigeons.

SACR

Sandhill Crane

Antigone canadensis

FIELD MARKS

- Red forehead
- Gray overall
- Black legs
- Bustle of drooping tail feathers

HABITAT
Meadows, prairies, fields, and wetlands

DIET
Seeds, fruits, insects, amphibians, and small mammals

NEST
Cup of twigs and stems on a large mound of vegetation

CALLS & SONGS
Loud, rattling bugle

RANGE

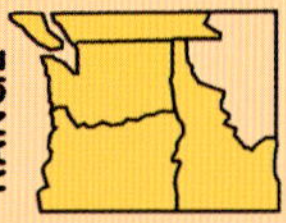

SIZE XL

Length ~45"
Wingspan ~75"

This huge bird is almost 4 feet tall with a wingspan of more than 6 feet, and it has a voice to match. You can hear a Sandhill Crane's loud, rattling bugle call from far away. A beginning birder might confuse this bird with the Great Blue Heron. Look for its red forehead patch and feathers that hang down over the tail, called a bustle. Unlike Great Blue Herons, Sandhill Cranes usually gather in large groups to fly or to feed on the ground. To impress one another, they bow, stretch their wings, and leap into the air. And they also use props, often picking up sticks and tossing them into the air.

Sandhill Cranes dancing

DID YOU KNOW?

A Sandhill Crane chick, called a colt, is a great example of a precocial bird. These chicks hatch with downy feathers and open eyes, and they're ready to move around on their own almost immediately after hatching. Some birds, like many songbirds, are altricial. They're born naked and blind and need to spend a few weeks in the nest being tended by parents before they're ready to be independent.

SHOREBIRDS

Not all birds at the shore are shorebirds, and not all shorebirds live at the shore. In general, birders use the word *shorebird* to describe many small birds such as sandpipers and plovers that feed along the edges of the water. You'll often find shorebirds at the beach, on a nearby mudflat, or in a wetland. But a few shorebirds live in forests and even grasslands. They vary in size from small sandpipers, sometimes called "peeps," that are just a few inches tall, to the Long-billed Curlew, whose bill is 8 inches long.

BNST

Black-necked Stilt

Himantopus mexicanus

FIELD MARKS
- Long, thin black bill
- Long, pink legs
- White forehead and eye patch

HABITAT
Shallow lakes, wetlands, and open mudflats

DIET
Aquatic invertebrates, small fish, and snails

NEST
Shallow depression on a clump of vegetation, lined with grass, mud, or shells

CALLS & SONGS
Sharp, loud *keek-keek-keek!*

RANGE

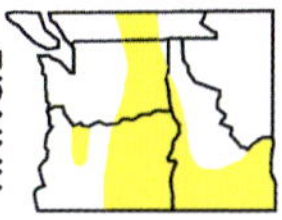

SIZE M

Length ~15"
Wingspan ~28"

This black-and-white shorebird has long, pink legs and a thin, black bill. Often seen alongside avocets, they're found in warmer months, wading through shallow water and probing for aquatic invertebrates. A group of stilts may circle a predator and leap up and down, flapping their wings to scare the animal away. They're protective of their nest sites and make a sharp *keek-keek-keek* if disturbed. They also do distraction displays to distract a predator: they sit on the ground away from their actual nest site, pretending to incubate eggs. Or they pretend to be injured, flying a short distance and repeating the display, to draw predators away from their nests.

DID YOU KNOW?
Black-necked Stilts and American Avocets (next page) have a lot in common and are often seen together. They both like to wade through shallow lakes and find aquatic invertebrates to eat. They can even mate and have babies that are a hybrid of the two species. These hybrids have been called "avostilts" by some scientists and "stavocets" by others. Which name do you think is a better fit for this unusual bird hybrid?

AMAV

American Avocet

Recurvirostra americana

FIELD MARKS

- Long, thin, upturned bill
- Pinkish tan head and neck
- Long, gray legs

HABITAT
Shallow lakes, wetlands, and open mudflats

DIET
Aquatic invertebrates and insects

NEST
Shallow scrape sometimes lined with grass, feathers, or pebbles

CALLS & SONGS
High *wheek-wheek-wheek*

RANGE

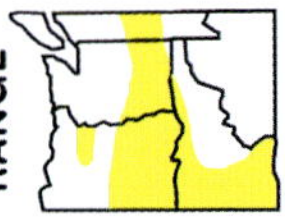

SIZE M

Length ~18"
Wingspan ~30"

This large shorebird has a long, thin, and slightly upturned bill; a black-and-white body; and a beautiful pinkish tan head and neck. It is often seen foraging and resting alongside Black-necked Stilts in shallow waterways during summer. Most shorebirds use their bills to probe into the ground for food, but avocets wade through shallow water, sweeping their bills from side to side to stir up and grab aquatic insects. This feeding behavior is known as scything, named for the farm tool that's swung back and forth to cut grass or harvest crops. With its upturned bill, long and spindly legs, and unusual feeding behavior, the American Avocet is an elegant bird and a favorite for many birders.

DID YOU KNOW?

Avocets nest directly on the ground, usually out in the open, on or near shallow water. When there is no shade at a nest site, an avocet sometimes dips its belly in the water before sitting atop its eggs to keep the eggs from overheating. If the area floods, American Avocets will build up their nests 12 inches or more using sticks, bones, and feathers to keep their eggs safe and above water.

BLOY

Black Oyster-catcher

Haematopus bachmani

FIELD MARKS

- Long, reddish orange bill
- Yellow eyes ringed in red
- Thick, pinkish legs

HABITAT
Rocky shorelines

DIET
Mollusks like mussels and clams

NEST
Shallow depression on rocks or sand

CALLS & SONGS
Loud, piping call notes and a rising *whee!*

RANGE

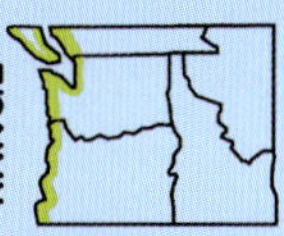

SIZE

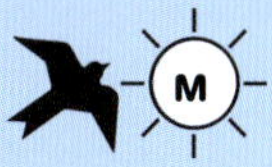

Length ~17"
Wingspan ~32"

Next time you're at the coast, scan a rocky area with your binoculars and look for this chunky, dark shorebird with a carrot for a bill. The Black Oystercatcher has a long, reddish orange bill that it uses to pry open clams and mussels and to probe the sand for worms and invertebrates. Even though they're large with brightly colored bills, they blend in with dark, rocky shorelines and can be tough to spot if they're not moving. When an oystercatcher moves, you'll hear its loud piping calls or strange *whee!* call. Try to get a closer look and notice its pinkish legs and bright yellow eyes.

DID YOU KNOW?

Many bird species that live in the western part of North America are similar, and often closely related, to species found in the eastern part. Some physical similarities are obvious: the Western Bluebird, for example, looks a lot like its cousin, the Eastern Bluebird. Other similarities can cause confusion: people in the eastern part of the continent see Blue Jays at their feeders, but our blue-feathered jays are usually Steller's Jays or California Scrub-Jays. On the east coast, American Oystercatchers have a white belly and a brown back, but they act a lot like our Black Oystercatchers.

KILL

Killdeer

Charadrius vociferus

FIELD MARKS

- Double black breast bands
- Long tail and wings
- Dark eyes with red eye rings

HABITAT
Open areas—fields, mudflats, lawns, parking lots, and airports

DIET
Mostly invertebrates like insects and worms; also seeds

NEST
Shallow scrape in the bare ground, sometimes lined with rocks, shells, or sticks

CALLS & SONGS
High, piercing *kill-deer, kill-deer* and *dee-dee-deer*

RANGE

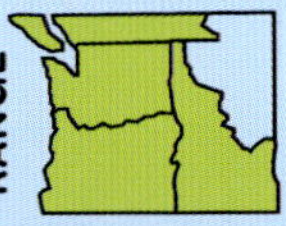

SIZE S

Length ~10"
Wingspan ~24"

This shorebird is named for its high-pitched, piercing *kill-deer, kill-deer, kill-deer* call. It prefers to live in wetlands, farm fields, and grassy parks near the beach, but it can be found almost anywhere that's flat and open, even in parking lots and neighborhoods. It's brown on top and white underneath, with a distinct double black band across its breast. Killdeer often stand or walk out in the open, calling loudly, and are easy to spot. They nest out in the open and are known to lay eggs right on busy footpaths, on active driveways, and in other places that don't seem like great nesting spots. And they don't need to build much of a nest because their eggs are well camouflaged and resemble rocks. When a predator approaches a Killdeer's nest site, the Killdeer will droop a wing down toward the ground and fan its tail, pretending to be injured. Then it will start moving away from the nest to lure the predator away. This bird can put on a pretty convincing show!

SEMIPALMATED PLOVER

Looks like a miniature Killdeer, but it has one black band across its belly instead of two.

BLACK-BELLIED PLOVER

(BREEDING)

Has striking breeding plumage, with a black belly and face.

Plain and gray in winter. They make a loud *kee-err-wee* call that rises and falls.

BLACK-BELLIED PLOVER

(WINTER)

SNOWY PLOVER

Tiny and sand-colored and can be hard to spot on a beach or a dried lakebed. You may see signs at the beach about staying away from nest sites to help protect this bird, which struggles to live alongside people.

Other Shorebirds

Shorebirds can be tough to identify, even for experienced birders. Many are small, fast-moving, and seen only from far away. Field marks may make them easier to spot, and some can be identified based on where they are or how they move. When shorebirds are part of a large mixed flock, you need time, patience,

SANDERLING

Clean white belly, grayish back, and white wing stripe visible when it flies; usually in flocks, running along the beach

LEAST SANDPIPER

Smallest shorebird in the Northwest, with yellowish legs

PECTORAL SANDPIPER

Looks like a large Least Sandpiper, but with a streaky breast that ends in a straight line above a white belly

WESTERN SANDPIPER

Slightly larger than Least Sandpiper, with a longer, droopier bill and black legs

WHIMBREL

Large, with a long, downcurved bill and dark crown stripes

MARBLED GODWIT

Tall and hefty, with a very long, slightly upturned bill

and experience to identify all the birds present. Birders who are good at identifying shorebirds remember detailed field marks, such as leg color, bill shape, feather patterns, and wing length, and they remember different calls.

Learn the most common birds in your area and pay attention to field marks or behaviors that set a species apart from the others. You might then recognize a rare or unusual bird by noticing how it differs from those you commonly see.

SURFBIRD

Looks like the Black Turnstone, with a thicker and stubbier-looking bill, plain gray plumage, and spotted belly

DUNLIN

Medium-sized, with a long and drooping bill, short legs, and a dark belly patch in summer

RUDDY TURNSTONE

Patchy black, white, and reddish plumage, orange legs, and a short, dark bill; usually forms small groups on rocky shores

BLACK TURNSTONE

Similar in shape and size to the Ruddy Turnstone but with a black head, back, and breast and a white belly

WILLET

Grayish, with a straight bill and black-and-white-patterned wings

WANDERING TATTLER

Dark gray, with yellow legs; found in rocky places

Long-billed Curlew

Numenius americanus

FIELD MARKS
- Superlong, down-curved bill
- Superlong, gray legs
- Plain belly

HABITAT
Grasslands and fields in summer; wetlands and mudflats in winter

DIET
Insects, crustaceans, and small invertebrates

NEST
Small scrape in the ground, lined with pebbles, plants, and sticks

CALLS & SONGS
Loud *ka-ree* calls that rise at the end and repeated high-pitched *prip-prip-prip!*

RANGE

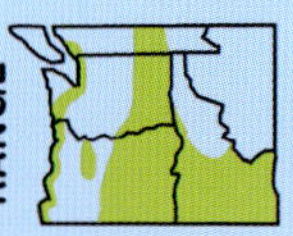

SIZE

Length ~24"
Wingspan ~33"

This curlew's incredibly long bill is very thin and curves downward. It's the largest shorebird we see in the Northwest and is a beautiful cinnamon color, with a heavy body, a long neck, and a small, round head. It breeds in grasslands but is often seen in wetlands or at the beach during migration. New birders may be surprised when they see this shorebird out in open grassland, far from the shore. When nesting, Long-billed Curlews are aggressive and will even gang up on hawks and coyotes that get too close. They make loud *ka-ree* calls that rise at the end and a series of high-pitched *prip-prip-prip* calls.

DID YOU KNOW?
During migration, Long-billed Curlews can be seen foraging in mudflats along the coast with other shorebirds like Willets and Marbled Godwits. Shorebirds are often far away and moving around constantly, making them hard to identify. But some of these larger shorebirds, especially when they're in a mixed flock, are a bit easier. Identifying a Marbled Godwit, with its long, two-toned bill, is a bit easier when it's next to a larger Long-billed Curlew, with its longer, downcurved bill, or a smaller Willet, with its stubbier bill.

WISN

(BNFB)

Wilson's Snipe

Gallinago delicata

FIELD MARKS
- Striped head
- Long, thick bill
- Barring on flanks

HABITAT
Wet, marshy areas

DIET
Insects and small invertebrates

NEST
Scrape in the dirt, lined with grass

CALLS & SONGS
Skape call when flushed and sharp *tik* calls

RANGE

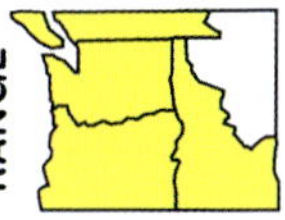

SIZE S

Length ~10"
Wingspan ~18"

This common shorebird can be extremely difficult to spot because of its excellent camouflage. For most of the year, these plump, long-billed birds hide in marshes. You might see one probing its long bill into the muck at the water's edge as it looks for food. Or you might flush one accidentally and watch it zigzag away over the wetland. If you're lucky, you'll see a Wilson's Snipe do its winnowing courtship display on a spring or summer night. During the display, the snipe circles high overhead, and the air moving through its outspread tail feathers makes a strange, whirring *huh-huh-huh-huh* sound. It's a sound, and a sight, you will not forget!

LONG-BILLED DOWITCHER

Dowitchers have plump bodies and long, sturdy bills like snipes, but their legs are much longer. Long-billed and Short-billed Dowitchers live in the Pacific Northwest. Their names aren't helpful, since they have similar-sized bills and look almost identical. In fact, the best way to tell the two apart is by their calls. The Long-billed makes high *keet, keet* calls and the Short-billed makes low, soft *too-too-too* calls.

SPSA

Spotted Sandpiper

Actitis macularius

FIELD MARKS

- Spotted belly
- White eyebrow
- Orange bill

HABITAT	DIET	NEST	CALLS & SONGS
Along rivers and streams	Small invertebrates, insects, worms, and snails	Scrape in the soil, lined with plants	*Peet-weet* calls; song is repeated *churee!*

RANGE

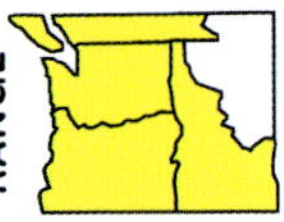

SIZE

S

Length ~8"
Wingspan ~15"

This sandpiper bobs up and down almost constantly. The behavior, often called teetering, makes this bird easy to identify from far away. Unlike some of our other sandpipers, a "spotty" is not usually found at the beach and doesn't travel in a large flock. Instead, it walks alone along a river or stream or flies out across open water. In winter, its belly is white and its upperparts are brown; in summer, its belly is spotted and its bill is orange. This sandpiper is typically quiet until it's flushed; then it lets out a repeated *peet-weet* call as it flies low over the water with its signature quick, stiff wingbeats and short glides.

DID YOU KNOW?

With most bird species, the male claims and defends a territory. But Spotted Sandpipers have an unusual mating system. During the breeding season, the female defends a territory and the male incubates the eggs and takes care of the chicks!

GRYE

Greater Yellowlegs

Tringa melanoleuca

FIELD MARKS
- Long, thin bill
- Long, yellow legs
- Streaky breast
- White belly

HABITAT
Marshes, flooded fields, and mudflats

DIET
Aquatic invertebrates

NEST
Shallow bowl in soft ground, lined with leaves or lichen

CALLS & SONGS
Three loud notes—*tew-tew-tew!*

RANGE

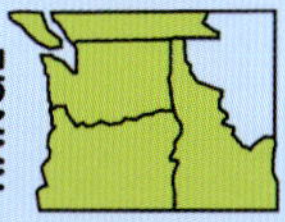

SIZE M

Length ~12"
Wingspan ~26"

This bird looks like a large sandpiper when you spot it, but you'll probably find it in a marsh or flooded field instead of on a sandy beach. As its name suggests, the Greater Yellowlegs has long, bright yellow legs and is larger than its look-alike, the Lesser Yellowlegs. You'll usually see this bird walking or wading along, grabbing at small invertebrates with its long, thin bill. When flushed, it flies quickly and directly while calling a series of three high notes—*tew-tew-tew!*

LESSER YELLOWLEGS

Looks like a smaller version of the Greater Yellowlegs, but the two can be difficult to tell apart. Since they're not always side by side, the best field mark to use is the bill length. The bill of the Greater Yellowlegs is much longer than its head. The bill of the Lesser Yellowlegs is about the same length as its head. When the two birds are side by side, the size difference is obvious, but when the birds are alone it can be hard to judge.

WIPH

(BNFB)

Wilson's Phalarope

Phalaropus tricolor

FIELD MARKS

- Dark eye and neck stripe
- Peach-colored neck
- White throat and eyebrows
- Very thin bill

HABITAT
Marshes and shallow wetlands

DIET
Aquatic invertebrates

NEST
Small bowl of plant material near water

CALLS & SONGS
Series of short *quip* notes

RANGE

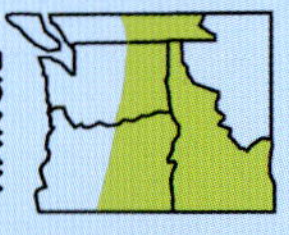

SIZE S

Length ~9"
Wingspan ~16"

Though these tiny birds aren't usually seen at the shore, phalaropes (FA-ler-opes) are considered shorebirds. Our three phalarope species are more likely to be either far out at sea or inland in shallow pools. They have long legs, pointed wings, and thin, straight bills. All three species share a unique feeding habit: Instead of running along the water's edge like typical shorebirds, they often spin around and feed in the water. They swim in small, tight circles and make a little whirlpool. This whirlpool draws insects and crustaceans up from deeper water so the bird can pluck them from the water's surface. Look for Wilson's Phalaropes in sewage ponds or shallow wetlands. Female phalaropes are larger and more colorful than males. The smaller, duller males are in charge of incubating eggs and raising chicks. Females often mate with multiple males, and because the female is the first to migrate, she may leave several males behind to incubate eggs and care for chicks on their own!

RED-NECKED PHALAROPE
(WINTER)

Can look like Wilson's Phalaropes but are smaller and darker overall in summer. In winter, they're pale with black ear patches.

RED PHALAROPE
(WINTER)

Bright red in summer, with a white face and a yellow bill. In winter, they're white with dark smudges near their eyes. They have a thicker bill than the other phalaropes and usually stay far out at sea. Sometimes winter storms will push them inland.

SEABIRDS

These marine birds spend most or all of their lives out on the ocean. They usually nest in big groups on the coast or on islands close to shore. Some of them are coastal year round, meaning they stay close to land, and others are pelagic, which means they spend almost their whole lives out on the open ocean. Some seabirds, like loons, spend winters out at sea but breed far inland on lakes. Some seabirds are known for incredibly long migrations that take them to many of the world's oceans.

TUPU

Tufted Puffin

Fratercula cirrhata

FIELD MARKS

- Long, yellow head tufts
- Orange bill and legs
- White face

HABITAT
Feeds far out at sea; nests on rocky islands

DIET
Mostly small fish

NEST
Made of plant material, deep in a burrow or hidden in rocks

CALLS & SONGS
Low growls and purrs while at nesting colony

RANGE

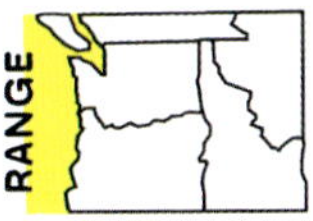

SIZE M

Length ~15"
Wingspan ~25"

One of our most colorful seabirds can be seen along the coast from April to August. A Tufted Puffin has a black body, a white face, a giant orange bill, and orange feet. In summer, its long, yellow tufts flop down the back of its head. It spends most of its time out fishing in the open ocean. Its massive bill can carry more than 20 fish at a time back to its hungry pufflings—an adorable name for baby puffins. You might spot this colorful bird standing near its burrow on a rocky island close to shore or flying in from the ocean with a bill full of fish.

RHINOCEROS AUKLET

A less colorful cousin of the Tufted Puffin. Has a white "horn" that grows from its beak, long white eyebrows, and a white mustache to match.

MAMU

Marbled Murrelet

Brachyramphus marmoratus

FIELD MARKS

- Black cap and upperparts
- White underparts
- White patch on wings

HABITAT
Close to shore on the ocean and in old-growth coastal forests

DIET
Small fish

NEST
None! Eggs are laid on a mossy branch or in an old bird or squirrel nest

CALLS & SONGS
High, loud *keeer*

RANGE

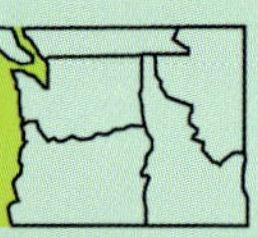

SIZE

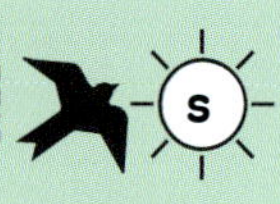

Length ~9"
Wingspan ~16"

For a long time, this bird's nesting habits were a mystery to scientists. It spends its time floating and feeding on the ocean, sometimes close to shore. But it doesn't nest on the rocks or cliffs along the coast like many other seabirds. Finally, scientists found a Marbled Murrelet nest—and it was in a tree, miles from the ocean! It turns out these birds spend most of their time feeding on the ocean, but they lay their eggs high in trees on moss-covered branches, sometimes deep in the forest and many miles from the water. In fact, they prefer to nest in old-growth forests, where the trees are more than 200 years old! Unfortunately, there aren't many of these trees or forests left in the Pacific Northwest. As a result, the Marbled Murrelet is considered an endangered species, which means it's in trouble.

DID YOU KNOW?

The Marbled Murrelet is a great example of a bird that changes its look depending on the time of year. This is because many birds molt (lose older feathers and grow new ones) into breeding plumage during spring and summer when they're mating and laying eggs, and then they molt again into nonbreeding plumage for fall and winter. Marbled Murrelets have chocolate-brown feathers during the breeding season and black-and-white plumage in winter.

COMMON MURRE

Looks similar to a Marbled Murrelet but is much larger, with a darker back and a larger bill.

PIGEON GUILLEMOT

Larger and almost all black, except for a white wing patch.

Gulls

Many birders cringe when they hear someone incorrectly call a bird a "seagull." That's because the bird in question is properly called a gull. There are more than 40 species of gulls, and some do live at the sea, but many live inland too. Some gulls are the size of small doves, while others are as big as ospreys!

Gulls change their look throughout the year, with different plumage during the breeding season and the nonbreeding season. Gulls also change their plumage during the first few years of their lives. Many gull species look very similar to one another and identifying them can be tough. Even experienced "gullers" will sometimes look at a gull with unique plumage, or one that's a hybrid of two gull species, and admit that they aren't sure exactly what they're looking at. But some birders love that challenge. To learn to identify gulls, start by noticing the differences among the most common gulls in your area. Look at things like head and bill shapes and the colors of the back, wingtips, and legs.

BONAPARTE'S GULL (BNFB)

Tiny gull with black head in summer and a black spot behind each eye in winter

FRANKLIN'S GULL (BNFB)

Often found far inland, with a dark hood and a broken white eye ring

HEERMANN'S GULL (BNFB)

Unique looking gull with a dark gray body, clean white head, and bright red bill; visits our coast in summer

SHORT-BILLED GULL

Small gull with a round and pigeonlike white head, a thin bill, and yellow legs

RING-BILLED GULL

Often found in towns and cities; has yellow legs and a dark ring around its yellow bill

CALIFORNIA GULL

White head, gray back, yellow legs, dark eyes, and yellow bill often with red spot near the tip

WESTERN GULL

Large coastal gull with a dark back, pink legs, and a plain white head

HERRING GULL

Large gull usually seen in winter, with a streaky pale head and pale eyes

GLAUCOUS-WINGED GULL

Very common, with pale gray wings (*glaucous* means gray), pink legs, and thick yellow bill

BLACK-LEGGED KITTIWAKE

Small gull that spends most of its life at sea, with black feet and black wingtips

Caspian Tern

Hydroprogne caspia

HABITAT
At the coast, along lakes and rivers

DIET
Mostly fish

NEST
Shallow scrape in the open, ringed by pebbles and shells, lined with plant materials

CALLS & SONGS
Harsh, gravelly *kow*; juveniles beg for food with a weak *ree-ooh* whistle

RANGE

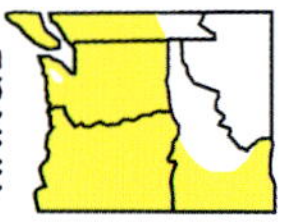

SIZE L

Length ~21"
Wingspan ~50"

This heavy-looking seabird with an oversized head is the world's largest species of tern. It has a black crown, black wingtips, and a pointy red bill. You may see this bird flying over saltwater or freshwater habitats with its bill pointed down as it scans for fish to dive after. When it spots something, it plunges into the water headfirst and grabs its meal with that thick, red bill. Sometimes Caspian Terns rest alongside other terns and gulls near water. They're notoriously defensive of their eggs and chicks. If you happen upon a breeding colony of Caspian Terns in a salt marsh or along a lake or river, the birds will dive bomb you until you move along. Young birds are fed by their parents for months after they fledge (or leave) their nests. It takes a long time for them to learn how to fish for themselves, so it's not uncommon to see what looks like a fully grown Caspian Tern following its parents around, loudly begging for food.

FIELD MARKS
- Black crown
- Thick, pointy red bill
- Black wingtips, legs, and feet

BLACK TERN

A tiny, all-dark tern that hunts for insects and small fish by flying over freshwater pools with incredible twists, turns, and swoops.

COMMON TERN

Smaller than the Caspian Tern. It has a long, thin, red bill with a black tip and long wings that stick out way past its tail when folded back.

FORSTER'S TERN (BNFB)

Another smaller tern that's found mostly inland, on fresh water. It can look very similar to a Common Tern but has gray instead of black wingtips.

COLO

Common Loon

Gavia immer

FIELD MARKS

- Heavy, pointed bill
- Black, blocky head
- Checkerboard back

HABITAT
Breeds on lakes; winters close to coast or on large waterways

DIET
Mostly fish

NEST
Mound of plant material at the edge of a lake

CALLS & SONGS
Strange, eerie tremolo (short, wavering call), yodel, and wail

RANGE

SIZE L

Length ~32"
Wingspan ~46"

This large waterbird is famous for its bizarre yodeling calls, haunting wails, and underwater dives that can last for several minutes at a time. It's best identified by its heavy, daggerlike bill, its blocky head, and its low profile on the water. In summer, Common Loons breed inland on a few lakes in the Northwest, but we are far more likely to see them in winter, floating in rivers or on the ocean.

COMMON LOON (WINTER)

DID YOU KNOW?

Loons are notorious for needing a long runway to get airborne. These birds will run across the top of the water, flapping their wings, sometimes for up to a quarter of a mile before they can get up into the air—that's the same distance as a full lap around most tracks! Common Loons have been known to get stuck on small waterways if they land there to rest but find there isn't enough room for a takeoff!

RED-THROATED LOON

(WINTER)

Not usually in their breeding plumage when they're visiting the Northwest, so they won't have their signature red throat. Instead, you can identify this loon by its smaller, thinner bill and the way it tends to hold it up at an angle.

PACIFIC LOON

(WINTER)

Smaller than the Common Loon, with a rounder gray head and a thinner bill. In winter, this loon has a dark chinstrap on its neck.

Pelagic Birds

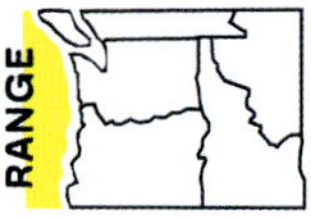

Some seabirds are difficult to find unless you're in a boat on the water. Pelagic birds spend most of their lives at sea and rarely come to land. Even though you're far more likely to see these birds from a boat, you might get lucky and see one that flies close to shore, especially if you spend time at the beach or on a jetty. Big storms can also bring some pelagic species close to shore, or even inland.

PARASITIC JAEGER

One of three look-alike species of jaegers in the Northwest, is a famously fast-moving cousin of gulls and known for being kleptoparasitic—they steal food caught by other animals, usually other birds like terns and gulls

BLACK-FOOTED ALBATROSS

Dark with white ring around its long, thick bill; like most albatross, famous for its large wingspan, effortless flight, and long life spent at sea

LAYSAN ALBATROSS

White head and a pink bill; glides over the ocean surface with minimal effort thanks to its incredible wingspan

FORK-TAILED STORM-PETREL

Tiny seabird that dances on the surface of the water as it feeds

NORTHERN FULMAR

Common seabird with long wings and a strange, broken-looking bill

SOOTY SHEARWATER

Most common shearwater in the Northwest is dark gray-brown, flies and glides over the surface of the ocean with stiff wings; known for incredibly long migration path

DCCO

Double-crested Cormorant

Nannopterum auritum

HABITAT
Along the coast and on larger waterways inland

DIET
Mostly fish

NEST
Big stick nest that incorporates found objects, even trash

CALLS & SONGS
Usually quiet, but sometimes makes piglike grunts

RANGE

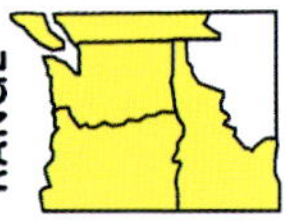

SIZE

Length ~32"
Wingspan ~53"

This large, dark waterbird doesn't have waterproof feathers, so it's often seen perched near the water, holding up its wings to dry in the sun. If they're not drying off on land, Double-crested Cormorants can be spotted swimming along and diving for fish. Cormorants often swim with only their head and S-shaped neck above the water. This bird's name makes more sense in summer, when it has two curly black or white crests on its head. Cormorants are considered seabirds, but Double-crested Cormorants can live almost anywhere with deep water. They build big stick nests in large colonies along waterways and are often seen on rivers and lakes in cities. Two other cormorant species are commonly found in the Pacific Northwest—the Brandt's Cormorant and the Pelagic Cormorant—but they are almost always found on the coast.

FIELD MARKS
- Orangish throat patch and face
- Hooked bill
- Blue eyes

Double-crested Cormorant drying its wings

DID YOU KNOW?

From far away, the Double-crested Cormorant looks totally dark. But if you're able to get a closer look, you'll see that it has bright blue eyes. And if you're really lucky, it will open its bill. In summer, the inside of its mouth is also bright blue!

BRANDT'S CORMORANT (BNFB)

All black, and in summer, has a bluish throat pouch and wispy white feathers on its head.

PELAGIC CORMORANT

Smaller and darker overall, with a thinner bill and a blue-green iridescence to their feathers.

MARSHBIRDS

Several medium to large waterbirds can be spotted in marshy areas of the Pacific Northwest, including **pelicans, herons, egrets, and ibises**. Depending on where you live, some of these birds, like the Great Blue Heron or the Great Egret, are easy to find year round and often feed out in the open. They will even leave the marsh to hunt in open fields. Other marsh-birds migrate to our area and are seen only during the warmer months. Some, like the Green Heron and the American Bittern, prefer to stay hidden in the thick vegeta-tion of the marsh and can be hard to spot. A few of these birds, including the White-faced Ibis and the American White Pelican, like to move around in large flocks, and you can learn to spot them in the air from a great distance.

AWPE

American White Pelican

Pelecanus erythrorhynchos

FIELD MARKS
- White body
- Black wingtips
- Yellow-orange bill and pouch

HABITAT
Shallow wetlands and other bodies of water

DIET
Small fish

NEST
Large, shallow bowl scraped into sand or soil

CALLS & SONGS
Usually quiet, but grunts or croaks at nesting sites

RANGE

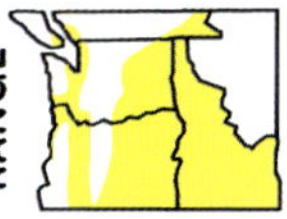

SIZE XL

Length ~62"
Wingspan ~105"

This huge white bird has a yellow-orange bill and pouch, and its wingtips are black. During the breeding season, adults have strange-looking horns growing atop their bills. Look for large flocks circling and soaring high in the air during migration. Or try to find these birds feeding in shallow wetlands, floating and scooping up small fish with their giant bills. Sometimes they tip forward to catch a fish, like a giant dabbling duck, and sometimes they work together to push a school of fish toward the shore before scooping them up. American White Pelicans begin life in an unusual way. At just a few weeks old, chicks leave their nests and form groups called creches (KRESH-iz).

BROWN PELICAN

The other pelican species found in the Northwest, the Brown Pelican, is found at the coast. They are grayish brown with yellow and white on the head and neck. Unlike the American White Pelican, which floats along and dips its bill to feed, the Brown Pelican soars over the ocean and then plunges into the waves to catch its meals.

American Bittern

Botaurus lentiginosus

FIELD MARKS
- Thick, pointy bill
- Brownish stripes
- Almost no tail
- Yellow legs

HABITAT
Marshes

DIET
Insects, crustaceans, fish, reptiles, amphibians, and small mammals

NEST
Mound of vegetation lined with grass, at the water's edge

CALLS & SONGS
Bizarre, gulping *pump-er-lunk* call and angry croak

RANGE

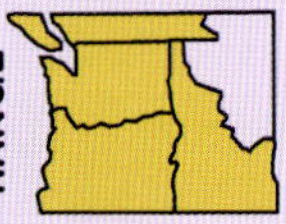

SIZE

Length ~28"
Wingspan ~42"

Looking for this bird in a marshy habitat is a bit like looking through an "eye spy" book. The American Bittern has excellent camouflage and often stands perfectly still, with its bill pointed upward, to blend in with the dried reeds and grasses in a wetland. This way of standing is called a concealment pose, and it helps the birds ambush, or sneak up on, prey. You might get lucky and see one walking slowly along the water's edge. But you're far more likely to hear this bird than to get a clear view of it. The males make bizarre, low *pump-er-lunk* calls that echo through marshes in spring.

DID YOU KNOW?

To make its signature *pump-er-lunk* call, the male American Bittern actually inflates his esophagus (a tube that moves food from its throat to its stomach). He opens and closes his bill, gulps in air, and then releases the trapped air. This watery, gulping sound echoes through the marsh and gives this bird a bunch of appropriately weird nicknames, including "thunder-pumper" and "water-belcher."

GBHE

Great Blue Heron

Ardea herodias

HABITAT
Freshwater and saltwater habitats, grasslands, and fields

DIET
Fish, reptiles, amphibians, small mammals, insects, and small birds

NEST
Bowl of plant material inside a large stick platform in a tree

CALLS & SONGS
Loud, croaky *thwaaak!*

RANGE

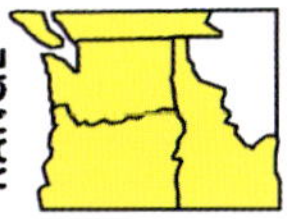

SIZE XL

Length ~46"
Wingspan ~72"

The largest heron in North America is commonly seen in our region. Great Blue Herons are patient, solo hunters that stalk prey while standing very still, before quickly snatching up a fish, snake, frog, or small mammal in their giant bill. It's quite a sight to see a Great Blue Heron swallow a snake, bullfrog, or rodent in one awkward gulp! They hunt in shallow wetlands or open fields. To spot one in the air, look for a large bird flying with slow, powerful wingbeats, its head tucked in tight and its feet trailing behind. When flushed, a Great Blue Heron makes a loud, croaky *thwaaak!* that sounds more like a dinosaur than a bird!

FIELD MARKS
- Long, pointed bill
- Long legs
- Dark plume of feathers on head
- Long, S-shaped neck

DID YOU KNOW?
Great Blue Herons have an unusual way of keeping clean. Special feathers on a heron's chest, called powder down, never stop growing. These small, downy feathers break up into a powder, and herons use a special claw on their middle toe to comb the powder into their feathers to clean them.

GREG

Great Egret

Ardea alba

FIELD MARKS
- Long, yellow bill
- Black legs and feet
- Long, curved neck

HABITAT
Freshwater and saltwater habitats, grasslands, and fields

DIET
Mostly small fish; also reptiles, amphibians, small mammals, birds, and invertebrates

NEST
Bowl made of plant material inside a large stick platform in a tree

CALLS & SONGS
Deep croaks; less vocal and quieter than Great Blue Heron

RANGE

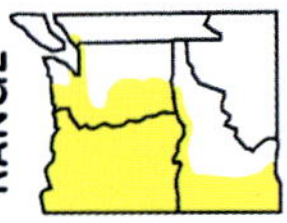

SIZE

Length ~38"
Wingspan ~50"

You can use the Great Egret's four-letter banding code as a fun nickname. Instead of telling your birding friends that a Great Egret is flying over, you can say, "GREG overhead!" Like its larger cousin, the Great Blue Heron, the Great Egret hunts slowly and patiently before jabbing its bill into water to catch prey. In summer, a patch of skin on the egret's face turns lime-green and long plumes grow from its back. These plumes are called aigrettes (AY-grets), not to be confused with the name of the birds (EE-grets). These feathers were once gathered and used to decorate ladies' hats, and this bird was hunted almost to extinction for those feathers!

SNOWY EGRET

The other white egret that you may see in the Pacific Northwest, though it's quite rare. It's smaller than the Great Egret and has a black bill and yellow feet.

WFIB

White-faced Ibis

Plegadis chihi

FIELD MARKS
- Reddish face outlined in white
- Long, down-curved bill
- Long, thin legs

HABITAT
Wetlands and fields

DIET
Mostly invertebrates like worms and insects

NEST
Platform of plants and sticks topped with a cup of plant material, in a tree or on the ground

CALLS & SONGS
Soft grunting sounds

RANGE

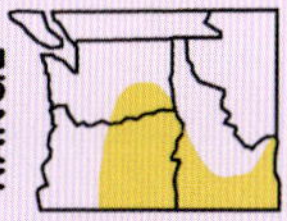

SIZE L

Length ~20"
Wingspan ~34"

With its long, downcurved bill and shiny, dark plumage, the White-faced Ibis is easy to identify from a great distance. In certain light, this bird may look completely dark, but its plumage can shimmer in greens, golds, and purples in the sun. Its name is slightly confusing, since this ibis doesn't really have a white face. Instead, it has a patch of pink skin in front of its eye, outlined in white. Look for a White-faced Ibis foraging in a marsh or field in the eastern parts of the Northwest. When a flock of White-faced Ibises flaps or glides by, you can identify them by their dark silhouettes, downcurved bills, and legs trailing behind.

DID YOU KNOW?

For its nest, the White-faced Ibis weaves a small platform out of plant stalks and builds a cup out of plant material on top. They use whatever plants are growing close to the nest site, and sometimes they come across other objects and include those too. Bits of litter, including plastic bags, hair combs, and empty shotgun shells, have been found inside the cups of White-faced Ibis nests.

GRHE

Green Heron

Butorides virescens

FIELD MARKS

- Dark cap
- Greenish back
- Brown-streaked neck
- Yellow legs

HABITAT
Wetlands

DIET
Mostly small fish

NEST
Stick nest in a tree

CALLS & SONGS
Loud, sharp *kyoo* and repeated *kow-kow-kow* calls

RANGE

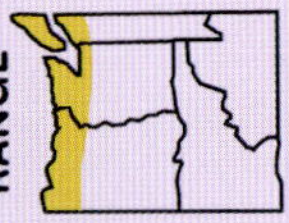

SIZE

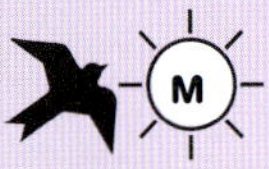

Length ~17"
Wingspan ~26"

This small and secretive heron can be hard to find, but it's worth the effort to see one. An expert at catching fish, it will drop insects or twigs onto the surface of the water to lure fish to the surface, where they're easier to grab! It's a very expressive, often silly-looking bird. Even when not hunting, a Green Heron can provide some serious entertainment by simply changing its head and neck positions. Sometimes, this heron will tuck in its long neck so much so that it seems to have no neck at all—then it will stretch its neck out and raise its shaggy crest. Look for a small, dark heron with yellow legs hunched in thick vegetation at the edge of the water, or listen for its sharp *kyoo* call as it flies out across the water.

Green Heron hunting

DID YOU KNOW?

Most birds have a pouch in their throat, called a crop, where they can store food. They may store food here before eating it, before feeding it to their young, or before they find a hiding place to save it for later. Birds don't chew their food because they don't have teeth like we do. Instead, birds have a gizzard, a special second stomach. Some birds eat bits of soil and rock, called grit, and these materials are stored in the gizzard. With the help of the rough grit, the gizzard squeezes and grinds up the food before it's digested.

BLACK-CROWNED NIGHT HERON

Another small, stocky heron that may be lurking around the edges of a wetland. This bird has a black crown and back, a white face and belly, and gray wings. It usually stays hidden away during the day because it prefers to forage at night.

RAPTORS & OWLS

The word *raptor* comes from a Latin word meaning "to seize," and it refers to birds like hawks and eagles that use their powerful feet to seize, or grab, their prey. Many birders also use the phrase "bird of prey" to describe any carnivorous (meat-eating) bird with strong eyesight, a sharp and curved beak, and sharp talons. These birds capture other animals for food. This section covers some of the birds of prey—**hawks, eagles, vultures, and owls**—that live in our region.

Not so long ago, many birds of prey were in serious trouble. A pesticide called DDT was making many birds' eggshells

too thin; they would crack easily so the babies inside couldn't survive. Thanks to major conservation efforts and the banning of DDT, populations of several species have bounced back and some have even been removed from the Endangered Species List.

Falcons aren't included here because they aren't closely related to these other birds of prey. Even experienced birders are surprised to learn that falcons are more closely related to parrots than they are to hawks or eagles! In this guide, falcons appear after the woodpeckers and before the flycatchers.

TUVU

Turkey Vulture

Cathartes aura

FIELD MARKS

- Small, bare, red head
- Pale legs
- Hooked bill

HABITAT
Open areas like farmland, forests, and high desert

DIET
Carrion

NEST
No nest; lays eggs on a cliff or in a cave, a dead tree, or an abandoned nest

CALLS & SONGS
Usually quiet; may grunt and hiss

RANGE

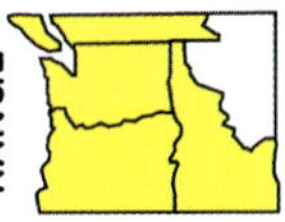

SIZE L

Length ~27"
Wingspan ~68"

Learn to recognize these large, dark birds as they soar high overhead, and you may spot them throughout spring and summer. A Turkey Vulture has a small, bare head, and its long wings are held in a shallow V-shape as it flies. It wobbles from side to side as it circles over an open area, riding on thermals, or currents of warm air. They often soar great distances without much flapping. Their flight feathers are grayish and almost see-through, which makes them stand out against dark wing feathers. Turkey Vultures are scavengers who eat mostly carrion, or dead animals. Without Turkey Vultures on clean-up duty, we'd see a lot more rotting roadkill along the highway!

DID YOU KNOW?

Turkey Vultures use their bodily fluids in some unusual and surprising ways! When a vulture needs to cool off on a hot day, it will poop on its own legs and feet. As the watery waste evaporates, it cools the vulture's skin. If you think that's gross, don't ever sneak up on an unsuspecting Turkey Vulture. When surprised or feeling threatened, this bird is known to vomit on whoever comes too close!

Osprey

Pandion haliaetus

FIELD MARKS

- White body
- Brown back
- Dark eye stripes and wrists

HABITAT
Near bodies of water with fish

DIET
Mostly fish

NEST
Large stick nest lined with bark and grass

CALLS & SONGS
High, whistled calls

RANGE

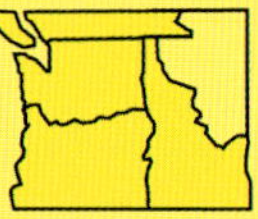

SIZE L

Length ~24"
Wingspan ~65"

Head to any good fishing spot on a large river, lake, or bay in the summer months and you're likely to see a large brown-and-white hawk fishing there too. Rightly nicknamed the "fish hawk," Osprey are known for plunging feetfirst into the water and pulling out large fish to eat. They're good at what they do and catch a fish in one out of every four attempts. You'll see them circling or hovering over the water and then diving down after a fish, with their talons out in front. Once an Osprey holds its catch in its talons, it uses a special toe to grip the fish and turn it so it faces forward, making it easier to carry. If you're watching an Osprey hunt, you'll probably also be able to find its huge stick nest nearby, built on a utility pole, a cell phone tower, pilings, or a special Osprey nesting platform.

DID YOU KNOW?

Birders often wow friends by identifying birds from a great distance, even if they see a bird for only a moment. That kind of skill can take time to learn, but knowing several distinguishing field marks for larger birds like raptors can make it easier for you to identify these birds. The next time you see an Osprey, pay special attention to the way its wing bends and the dark spots at the crook of that bend. This is the bird's wrist, and the shape is distinct in Ospreys, which makes them easier to identify from far away. You may see males high in the sky, performing aerial displays to impress females. Sometimes this display is called a sky dance or a fish flight. The male, holding a stick or a fish, will alternate between hovering in the air and swooping down and calling loudly.

WHITE-TAILED KITE

This white raptor is relatively new to the Northwest and its range is expanding. White-tailed Kites can be tough to spot in our area, but they're worth looking for along the coast of Oregon or Washington during fall and winter. It has intense red eyes and a bright white face, with a pale body and dark shoulder patches. Sometimes they fly low over the ground and other times they hover high overhead.

NOHA

Northern Harrier

Circus hudsonius

FEMALE NORTHERN HARRIER

FIELD MARKS

- Flat, owllike face
- Males: gray and white with black wingtips
- Females: brown with a darker head

HABITAT
Open grasslands and wetlands

DIET
Small mammals, especially voles; also reptiles, amphibians, and songbirds

NEST
Platform of plant stalks, lined with grass, in a clump of vegetation on the ground

CALLS & SONGS
Thin, whistled scream and angry *kek-kek-kek*

RANGE

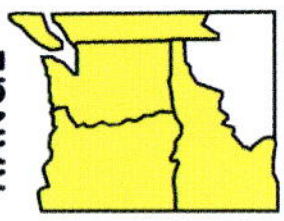

SIZE

Length ~19"
Wingspan ~43"

The male and female Northern Harrier both have a big white patch at the base of the tail and a flat, owllike face. Otherwise, they look completely different. The female is streaky brown and larger, while the male is pale gray with a white belly and dark wingtips. Watch as they hunt over open grassland. They tend to fly slowly and low over the landscape, with their wings held up in a V-shape, gliding and tilting as they look and listen for rodents on the ground. In winter, they often share open, grassy areas with Short-eared Owls, squabbling with them over the small rodents they both like to eat.

MALE NORTHERN HARRIER

DID YOU KNOW?

The eye colors of Northern Harriers change over the course of their lives. Young males have pale greenish eyes and young females have dark brown eyes. Adult birds have bright yellow eyes.

RTHA

Red-tailed Hawk

Buteo jamaicensis

FIELD MARKS

- Dark head
- Pale breast
- Dark belly band

HABITAT
Open areas with perches from which to hunt

DIET
Mostly mammals; also smaller birds, snakes, and carrion

NEST
Huge stick nest, lined with plant material, in a tall tree or on a cliff edge

CALLS & SONGS
Loud, raspy *KEY-errr!*

RANGE

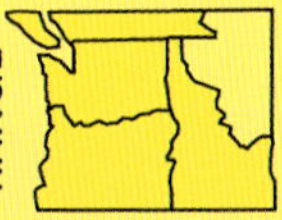

SIZE L

Length ~20"
Wingspan ~49"

If you see a hawk soaring over an open area or perched along the side of the road on a telephone pole, wire, or fence, chances are it's a Red-tailed Hawk. It's the most common hawk in the Northwest—but that doesn't mean it's always easy to identify. Red-tailed Hawks come in light morphs and dark morphs (a morph is the same species with a different color), and their plumage colors can vary. Adults in our region usually have a dark, streaky band across their belly and reddish tail feathers. When birders describe other hawks, they often compare them to Red-tailed Hawks, which are well known and easy to see in the Northwest.

DID YOU KNOW?

The Red-tailed Hawk's iconic call is a shrill and raspy *KEY-errr!* In TV shows and movies, this sound is often used for any raptor, including Bald Eagles. In reality, Bald Eagles make weak, high-pitched piping calls and nothing as majestic as the cry of a Red-tailed Hawk.

Forest Hawks

These hawks have short wings and long tails, and are known for a flight style of quick flaps and short glides. Until recently, these hawks were thought to be part of a group called "Accipiters." Scientists are learning that even though these birds are very similar, they aren't necessarily related. The forest hawks that live in the Pacific Northwest are Sharp-shinned Hawks, Cooper's Hawks, and American Goshawks. Sharp-shinned and Cooper's hawks look incredibly similar, and even if you use a field guide, it can be difficult to tell them apart. Birders sometimes argue about what species they're looking at! But even with a brief look, you may be able to identify each of these species confidently based on field marks. These forest hawks hunt and eat smaller birds and small mammals.

SHARP-SHINNED HAWK

Smaller hawk with a small head, dark cap that matches dark neck (making it look more like a dark hood), and thin legs

COOPER'S HAWK (BNFB)

Larger than Sharp-shinned Hawk, with a blockier head, dark cap, and longer, rounder tail

AMERICAN GOSHAWK

Largest forest hawk, with a gray back and a barred belly, requires huge areas of forest and is rarely seen close to urban places; once known as Northern Goshawk, but now acknowledged as two species: American Goshawk and Eurasian Goshawk

Other Hawks

Several medium to large hawks are found in the Pacific Northwest. But since the Red-tailed Hawk is the most common, it's helpful to learn how to identify that bird first. Once you're skilled at identifying Red-tailed Hawks, you're more likely to be able to identify these other hawks.

RED-SHOULDERED HAWK

Expanded its range into the Northwest and is becoming more common; smaller than Red-tailed Hawk, with reddish orange belly, black-and-white-checkerboard wing patterns, and black-and-white-striped tail

ROUGH-LEGGED HAWK

Winter visitor to Pacific Northwest has variable plumage color—from mostly white light morph to almost completely brown dark morph—with long and narrow wings, a long tail, a small bill, and feathers all the way down its legs

SWAINSON'S HAWK (BNFB)

Variable plumage in light and dark morphs, has long and pointed wings, usually white underwings, and dark flight feathers; usually seen in open, drier parts of the Northwest

FERRUGINOUS HAWK

Larger and usually paler than Red-tailed, but also comes in dark morphs; usually has white tail and white flight feathers with dark tips, feathered legs, and the base of its large beak is yellow

Bald Eagle

Haliaeetus leucocephalus

FIELD MARKS
- White head
- White tail
- Large, yellow bill

HABITAT
Forested areas, usually close to water

DIET
Mostly fish; also small birds, reptiles, amphibians, and small mammals and invertebrates

NEST
Enormous stick nest lined with grass and other soft material

CALLS & SONGS
High-pitched, shrill whistles

RANGE

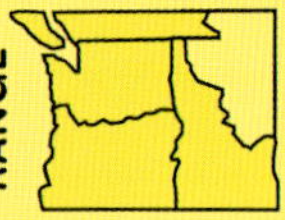

SIZE XL

Length ~34"
Wingspan ~80"

Everybody recognizes the Bald Eagle. As the national bird of the United States, it appears on our money, on T-shirts and hats, and is featured on television and in movies. In the 1960s, as populations declined, Bald Eagles were in serious trouble, but they were taken off the Endangered Species List in 2007 and are now doing well, especially in the Pacific Northwest. Even nonbirders can identify an adult Bald Eagle right away—with its dark body, white head and tail, and large yellow bill. Young Bald Eagles, however, can be hard to identify, because they're dark brown all over, sometimes with white patches on their wings, back, and tail. After a few years, their heads and tails start to look more whitish, but they don't develop the classic Bald Eagle colors until around their fifth birthday.

Bald Eagles hunting fish

DID YOU KNOW?

Juvenile Bald Eagles are often misidentified as Golden Eagles. For some reason, many people think Golden Eagles are larger than Bald Eagles, but they're actually about the same size. However, juvenile eagles (both Bald and Golden) can look larger than adults because a young eagle's tail and wing feathers are typically longer than those of adults. So when someone sees a juvenile Bald Eagle that is mostly dark brown and it looks bigger than a Bald Eagle, they mistakenly identify it as a Golden Eagle!

GOLDEN EAGLE

Brown overall with a golden nape, or back of the neck. These birds usually stay in remote, open country, away from people. Like Ferruginous and Rough-legged hawks, Golden Eagles have feathered legs. Juveniles have white patches on their wings and white at the base of their tail.

BANO

American Barn Owl

Tyto furcata

FIELD MARKS
- Smooth, rounded head
- White, heart-shaped face
- Dark eyes

HABITAT
Hunts in open areas; roosts in open buildings, caves, or tree cavities

DIET
Rats, mice, voles, shrews, bats, and sometimes birds

NEST
No nest!

CALLS & SONGS
Long, hissing, spooky shriek!

RANGE

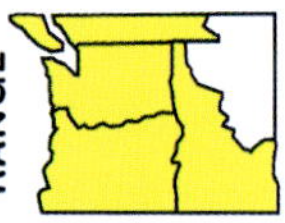

SIZE L

Length ~14"
Wingspan ~44"

The Barn Owl has rusty brown and gray feathers, a white face, dark eyes, and a short tail. Its belly can be white or cinnamon colored, and males are usually paler than females. They are nocturnal, or active at night, when they use their excellent vision and hearing to hunt. They fly with slow wingbeats, like giant moths flying past in the darkness. During the day, they roost in hollow trees, caves, or barns. Barn Owls don't make nests; instead, they lay eggs in hidden spots in caves, tree cavities, nest boxes, or barns.

DID YOU KNOW?

Even though Barn Owls have extremely good eyesight and can see in very little light, they rely on their excellent hearing to find prey. A Barn Owl will fly low over an open field, watching and listening for movement—it can detect a tiny mouse moving through grass, or even under the snow! Like other owls and birds of prey, Barn Owls eat their prey whole and later cough up a pellet made of the animal's fur and bones. You can look through an owl's pellet to learn more about its diet! Many birds of prey, like owls and falcons, produce pellets, but so do kingfishers, crows, shrikes, most shorebirds, and grebes.

GGOW

Great Gray Owl

Strix nebulosa

FIELD MARKS
- Giant, round face
- Ringed facial disc
- Black-and-white "bow tie" at throat

HABITAT
Mountain forests with meadows, bogs, or other open areas

DIET
Small mammals—voles, gophers, chipmunks, and mice

NEST
Old raptor or raven nests, human-made nesting platforms; may lay eggs directly into broken treetops

CALLS & SONGS
Deep, low hoots

RANGE

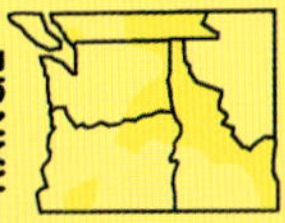

SIZE XL

Length ~27"
Wingspan ~56"

The largest owl in North America has a giant, round face and bright yellow eyes. Despite its enormous size, it weighs less than the much smaller Great Horned Owl because it's mostly feathers! It's very secretive and well camouflaged. When perched against the trunk of a tree, this owl can close its eyes or turn its head around and disappear into the patterns of the bark. In true owl fashion, it uses its excellent vision to spot small mammals from a great distance and its incredible hearing to track an animal's movement underground or through snow. Then it will float silently across the forest or meadow and drop onto its prey with open talons!

A Great Gray Owl blends in with tree bark

DID YOU KNOW?
Most owls owe their excellent hearing to their asymmetrical ear openings—this means that one ear is higher on the owl's head and one is lower. This helps the owl locate the source of sounds. Great Gray Owls are known to hear rodent prey scurrying around under several feet of snow, and they can even pounce on the exact right spot!

Great Horned Owl

Bubo virginianus

FIELD MARKS

- Large plumicorn ear tufts
- Large yellow eyes
- Brownish face

HABITAT
Places with open areas to hunt and spots to roost

DIET
Almost anything—rodents and small mammals, birds, and even other owls!

NEST
Takes over old hawk nests; also in tree cavities, on cliffs, and on platforms

CALLS & SONGS
Loud, deep, repeated *hoo-hoo-HOO, hoo-hoo!*

RANGE

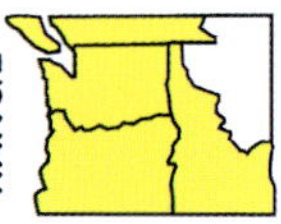

SIZE L

Length ~22"
Wingspan ~48"

Owls come in all shapes and sizes and make all sorts of noises. But the Great Horned Owl fits the classic idea of an owl—a large nocturnal predator with sharp talons and large yellow eyes set on a round, swiveling head. The "horns" on its head are actually tufts of feathers called plumicorns and have nothing to do with hearing (their ears are much farther down on the sides of their heads). It lives in a wide variety of habitats, and you're most likely to see one around sunset, perched on a tree, pole, or wire, looking and listening for its next meal. Sometimes it roosts in a tree during the daytime. Even if you don't get a chance to see this owl, there's a good chance you'll hear it if it's close by. Great Horned Owls give the classic owl call, usually at dusk and dawn. Listen for five deep hoots—*hoo-hoo-HOO, hoo-hoo!*—and you might hear another owl respond, as pairs often perform a duet.

DID YOU KNOW?

One of the best ways to find owls is to listen and watch when other birds are upset or angry. Because the Great Horned Owl is a predator of many birds, the birds react strongly and start "mobbing" the owl—they call loudly to get the attention of other birds and swoop at the owl and harass it until it moves along and finds a new place to be. Birds as large and loud as crows or as small and quiet as hummingbirds can lead you to a nearby owl!

LONG-EARED OWL

New birders sometimes think they've seen a Long-eared Owl when they've spotted a Great Horned Owl with particularly large or upright ear tufts. Remember that Long-eared Owls are much smaller and thinner than Great Horned Owls. Long-eared Owls have a streaked belly, an orange face with dark feathers around the eyes, and are much harder to find!

NOPO

Northern Pygmy-Owl

Glaucidium gnoma

FIELD MARKS

- Round head
- Yellow eyes
- White spots and speckles
- Long tail

HABITAT
Forested areas

DIET
Birds, small mammals, reptiles, and insects

NEST
Old woodpecker holes or other tree cavities

CALLS & SONGS
High, single *toot* notes, spaced a few seconds apart

RANGE

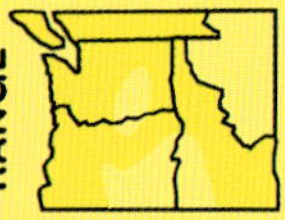

SIZE

Length ~7"
Wingspan ~15"

This tiny owl may seem cute, but it's known for being fierce. Northern Pygmy-Owls can kill prey several times their own size—and often do! Birders spot these miniature owls holding and eating sparrows, quail, and even large woodpeckers. It's a diurnal owl, meaning it's active during daylight hours. If you're walking deep in the woods and you hear a high-pitched *toot* that repeats every few seconds, follow this sound and try to spot this tiny predator. Or if you hear a group of chattering birds that sound angry, follow the sounds and you might see these birds ganging up and noisily harassing an owl, hoping to chase it away to avoid being caught for dinner! The Northern Pygmy-Owl has two dark markings on the back of its head that look like eyes—these are called ocelli (oh-SELL-ee). Some scientists think these spots confuse other birds about which way the owl is facing and keep the birds from attacking the back of the owl's head!

DID YOU KNOW?
Sometimes there is a certain species that a birder wants to see, but can't seem to find. When you've spent a long time looking for that species, or have been close to seeing it multiple times but haven't been able to, that species becomes your nemesis bird. A nemesis is a longtime enemy or rival. Some birders spend years trying to find their nemesis bird, and when they finally see it, it's cause for celebration. But it's also time to set their sights on a new nemesis bird!

WESTERN SCREECH-OWL

Another tiny owl, but unlike the Northern Pygmy-Owl, it's usually active in the evening. It has small ear tufts and makes a whistled "bouncy ball" song, where the notes speed up at the end of the song. This owl can be found in forests, but also in backyards and parks—even in the city!

BUOW

Burrowing Owl

Athene cunicularia

FIELD MARKS

- Round head
- Yellow eyes
- Short tail
- Long legs

HABITAT
Open areas—grasslands, deserts, and scrublands

DIET
Lizards, small birds, mammals, and invertebrates

NEST
Burrow up to several feet long and deep, with a small opening

CALLS & SONGS
Adults make chatter calls; males sing a sweet *coo*

RANGE

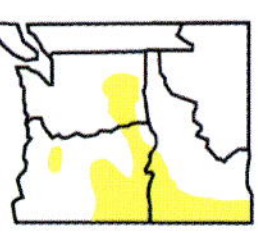

SIZE

Length ~9"
Wingspan ~21"

When you think of an owl, you probably think of a large predator that hides away in the forest during the day and hunts silently at night. But the Burrowing Owl does things a little differently. This small owl is about the size of a jay, and it's often active during the daytime. It lives in dry grasslands and deserts and, unlike most birds, nests in underground burrows. These long-legged, often grumpy-looking owls make their homes in the abandoned burrows of mammals like badgers. As you drive through open, dry country, you may see one perched on a fence post or standing on a mound of dirt near its burrow. If you ever find a burrow entrance, you'll notice that the owls have placed things like bottle caps, bits of metal, and paper scraps there, as well as animal dung they've collected. The dung attracts beetles and other critters that the owls eat, but the bits of trash seem to be Burrowing Owl home decorations!

DID YOU KNOW?

When a Burrowing Owl can't find an old mammal burrow to borrow, it has to improvise. Sometimes a pair of owls will nest in a concrete or plastic tube at a construction site or in a culvert that runs under a road. Burrowing Owl populations are declining in most areas because there are less burrowing mammals around to provide them with suitable homes. Conservationists working to save these owls build artificial burrows made of pipes, tubes, and buried buckets, and the owls move right in. To fool predators, owlets inside the burrow make a call that sounds like a rattlesnake. Imagine a predator digging around in a burrow, looking for a meal. If it hears that sound, it might be fooled and decide to move on!

BADO

Barred Owl

Strix varia

FIELD MARKS

- Dark eyes
- Barred breast and belly
- Gray face
- Yellow bill

HABITAT	DIET	NEST	CALLS & SONGS
Mixed forests	Rodents, mammals, amphibians, reptiles, and invertebrates	Tree cavity, another animal's abandoned stick nest, or nest box	Hoots, caws, cackles, and *Who-cooks-for-you? Who-cooks-for-you-all?* calls

RANGE

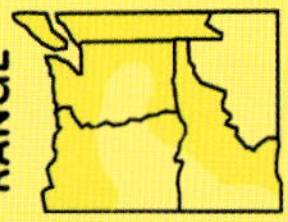

SIZE L

Length ~19"
Wingspan ~42"

Barred Owls are pretty new to the Pacific Northwest, having arrived here in the 1970s. These owls often live in city parks and will perch right by busy walking paths in our area. But not that long ago, this species lived only in the eastern parts of North America and wasn't in the Northwest at all. Because of development and tree planting in the middle of the country, Barred Owls began moving west. This has not been great news for the similar-looking Spotted Owl, a bird that's native to the Northwest and was already suffering population declines due to habitat loss. It turns out that the larger and more aggressive Barred Owl is making life harder for Spotted Owls. But despite its history and its effect on the beloved Spotted Owl, the Barred Owl is still exciting to see and hear while you're birding. Listen for its wild *Who-cooks-for-you?* call and keep your eyes peeled for this beautiful dark-eyed predator.

DID YOU KNOW?

Owls cannot move their eyes around like humans can. Instead, to look at something that's not directly in front of it, an owl turns its whole head. Owls are famous for this, and for good reason! They can turn their heads almost all the way around to keep an eye on things.

SPOTTED OWL

Smaller and less aggressive cousin to the Barred Owl and is native to the Pacific Northwest. It became a well-known species in the 1980s as a symbol of protecting forests from the uncontrolled logging practices that were destroying its habitat. Despite some moves to protect forest reserves, Spotted Owl populations continue to decline, in part because the Barred Owl's range has expanded into Spotted Owl territory. But the two species don't always compete, and sometimes they mate and produce hybrid babies called "sparred owls."

Other Owls

Owls are a delight to see, and many birders enjoy going owling (looking specifically for owls). Sometimes this means going out at night, but not always. Many owls can be seen at dusk and dawn, and a few can even be found in the middle of the day.

OWLETS

Finding an owl nest site is a special treat; owlets are especially entertaining to watch as they learn to climb and fly

GREAT HORNED OWLET

During branching, owlets move from the nest to branches before they can fly and sometimes lose their grip and hang awkwardly before falling to the ground and climbing back up the tree trunk

SNOWY OWL

All-white arctic species draws a lot of attention from birders and nonbirders when it visits a populated area in the Pacific Northwest

SHORT-EARED OWL

Has a slow, bouncy, mothlike flight pattern and makes delightful barking calls as it scans fields for voles; will hunt alongside and quarrel with Northern Harriers

NORTHERN SAW-WHET OWL

Tiny, nocturnal, hard-to-find owl prefers dense forests; named for its strange, squeaky calls that sound like saws being sharpened

FLAMMULATED OWL

Tiny mountain owl that nests in old woodpecker holes; difficult to see, but soft, deep *hoop* calls can be heard near rural, wooded campsites in summer

KINGFISHERS & WOODPECKERS

Many kinds of kingfishers live across the globe, and most have big heads, sharp bills, and short, stubby legs. They often hunt from perches, waiting and watching before swooping down on their prey. Some live near water and hunt for fish, while others live in the forest and hunt small animals. **Woodpeckers** are also found all around the world, usually in areas with plenty of trees. They have stiff tails that they use to prop themselves up on the sides of trees and can often be seen climbing up a trunk. They use their thick, pointy bills to peel bark or to dig out wood to uncover the insects they like to eat. Adults dig cavities in trees and tend to their young inside. Kingfishers and woodpeckers might not look like they're related, but they likely share a common ancestor.

BEKI

Belted Kingfisher

Megaceryle alcyon

FIELD MARKS

- Bushy crest
- Heavy, sharp bill
- Blue and rust-colored belly bands

HABITAT
Near rivers, ponds, lakes, and estuaries

DIET
Mostly small fish; also tadpoles, crayfish, insects, amphibians, and more

NEST
Tunnel-shaped burrow dug into a riverbank

CALLS & SONGS
Long, loud rattle

RANGE

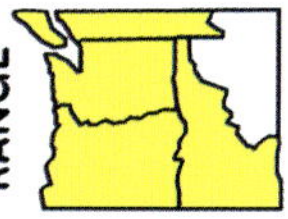

SIZE M

Length ~13"
Wingspan ~20"

With loud, rattling calls as it flies over waterways, the Belted Kingfisher is usually heard before it's seen. It looks down from its perch or hovers out over the water, watching for small fish. Then it dives in headfirst to catch its prey. If you're lucky, you'll see it whack its meal against a perch to stun it before swallowing it whole. This blue-and-white bird has a huge head with a bushy crest and a heavy bill. To know if you're seeing a male or a female, pay special attention to its belly: a male has one blue band across its belly, while a female has a blue band above a second, rust-colored band.

DID YOU KNOW?

The Belted Kingfisher has one giant toe claw on its foot that it uses to dig out its burrow in the bank of a stream or river. Burrows slope up and can be 8 feet deep! A pair of Belted Kingfishers will build a nest inside this tunnel-shaped burrow and defend the stretch of water nearby. If a new kingfisher starts fishing in a kingfisher's existing territory, you're going to hear about it! This bird's rattling call is loud, and the sound carries far.

ACWO

Acorn Woodpecker

Melanerpes formicivorus

FIELD MARKS

- Red crown
- Clownish face
- White eye and wing patch

HABITAT
Stands of mature oak trees

DIET
Acorns, of course; also insects, tree sap, and fruit

NEST
Cavity in a tree, no actual nest

CALLS & SONGS
Loud, goofy cackles and *waka-waka-waka* calls

RANGE

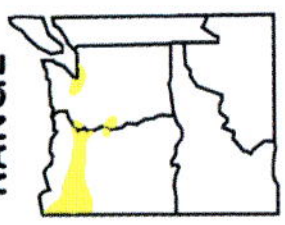

SIZE

S

Length ~9"
Wingspan ~16"

These clown-faced woodpeckers live in noisy family groups in areas with older oak trees. They're known for collecting acorns directly from the oak trees and storing them in dead tree limbs or dead trees, which are called granary trees. Acorn Woodpeckers chisel acorn-sized holes into the wood, and they fill each space perfectly with a single acorn. A granary tree can store hundreds of acorns for winter use and is often used year after year. Acorn Woodpeckers not only work together to gather and store food, but they also protect their granaries and care for their young cooperatively. They make loud, nasal *waka-waka-waka* calls that fit with their comical looks.

DID YOU KNOW?

Acorn Woodpeckers have very unusual and complicated family structures. More than a dozen birds may live together in a family group. They all work together to collect and store acorns and to protect their granary and the surrounding territory. Younger birds often stay with their parents and help care for the next few generations. In some families, multiple females lay eggs in a single nest and tend to their young together.

DOWO

Downy Woodpecker

Dryobates pubescens

FIELD MARKS

- Short, stubby bill
- Black-and-white face
- White belly
- Black back

HABITAT
Woodlands, parks, and backyards

DIET
Mostly insects; also fruits and seeds

NEST
Excavates a deep, wide cavity lined with wood chips

CALLS & SONGS
High, squeaky *pik* and high-pitched whinny

RANGE

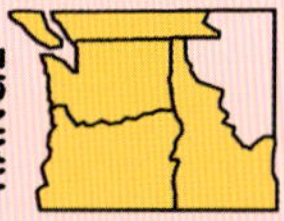

SIZE S

Length ~7"
Wingspan ~12"

The smallest woodpecker in North America and most common in our area, the Downy Woodpecker is a regular visitor to many backyard feeders. They often join other birds like chickadees and nuthatches in mixed flocks. This little woodpecker has a short, stubby bill. Paying attention to its size and bill will help you tell this bird apart from the very similar-looking, but much larger, Hairy Woodpecker. People are surprised to learn that woodpeckers can drill into trees to find insects without making much noise. When a woodpecker drums on a tree, mailbox, or the side of your house, it's more about making noise and getting the attention of other woodpeckers than about finding food.

HAIRY WOODPECKER

Look like larger versions of Downy Woodpeckers, and telling the two species apart can be tricky if they're not side by side, especially for new birders. Comparing the bill size to the size of the head is most helpful: On a Downy, the length of the bill is shorter than the width of the head. On the Hairy, the bill is as long as the width of the head. Hairy Woodpeckers also prefer evergreen forests and are less likely to visit a backyard feeder than Downy Woodpeckers.

RBSA

Red-breasted Sapsucker

Sphyrapicus ruber

HABITAT
Mixed forests

DIET
Sap, insects, spiders, fruits, and seeds

NEST
Excavates a deep cavity in dead wood

CALLS & SONGS
Squeaky *weet-weet-weet*, loud *wah-wah*, and bill drumming, *tat-a-tat-tat, tat, tat, tat*

RANGE

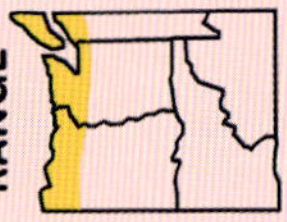

SIZE S

Length ~8"
Wingspan ~15"

Sometimes confused with Red-headed Woodpeckers, which live in the eastern part of the United States, this red-headed bird is common along the West Coast. It's part of the woodpecker family, but its name tells you something about its behavior. Sapsuckers drill shallow, tidy rows of holes in trees, called sap wells, and visit them regularly to feed on the sap that collects inside. Hummingbirds love sugary liquids and often drink from these sap wells too. Like most woodpeckers, the Red-breasted Sapsucker flies in an undulating pattern, rising as it flaps and falling slightly as it glides.

FIELD MARKS
- Red head and breast
- Pale belly
- White wing spots and wing patch

WILLIAMSON'S SAPSUCKER
(BNFB)

MALE

Males can look almost completely black when seen from a distance, but it has a red throat, a yellow belly, white wing patches, and white stripes on its face. This species tends to stay in drier forests in the eastern part of our region.

FEMALE

The female has a brown head and a light-colored, barred back.

RED-NAPED SAPSUCKER

Look similar to Red-breasted Sapsuckers but have black-and-white markings on their face.

DID YOU KNOW?

Ornithologists are always learning more about birds through research and genetic testing. Sometimes two birds that were considered separate species are discovered to be the same species, so they're lumped together. Or some birds that were considered a single species are determined to be two or more species, so these new species are split apart. At one time, the Red-breasted Sapsucker, the Red-naped Sapsucker, and a bird from eastern North America called a Yellow-bellied Sapsucker, were all thought to be the same species!

NOFL

Northern Flicker

Colaptes auratus

FIELD MARKS

- Long, pointed bill
- Black bib
- Spotted belly and striped back
- Male: gray face has red mustache

HABITAT
Woodlands, marshes, parks, and neighborhoods

DIET
Insects, especially ants and beetles, and fruits and seeds

NEST
Excavates a cavity in dead wood lined with wood chips

CALLS & SONGS
Call is a single, loud *key-ooh* and repeated *wick-a-wick-a-wick-a*; song is a loud rattle that rises and falls; drums a series of rapid taps

RANGE

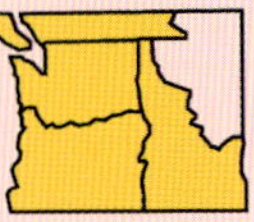

SIZE

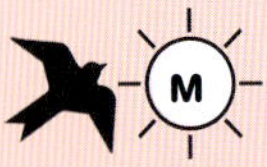

Length ~12"
Wingspan ~20"

This woodpecker is common in neighborhoods and is often a favorite of backyard birders. Most woodpeckers are black, white, and red, and most are seen climbing up the trunks of trees, but not Flickers! This brownish bird has dark bars on its back, black spots on its belly, and a black band on its breast. In flight, it flashes its bright orange-red wing feathers and white rump. The male Flicker has a bright red mustache. These woodpeckers love to eat ants and are just as likely to be seen feeding on the ground as they are to be perched on the side of a tree. When you learn to recognize this bird's loud *key-ooh* call, you'll hear it all over the place.

DID YOU KNOW?

When you see a Northern Flicker in flight, pay attention to the flash of color in its wings. Most Flickers in the Northwest are red-shafted, meaning their wings show a bright orange-red color. In eastern North America, yellow-shafted Flickers have yellow underwings. Scientists used to consider the two as separate species but now they lump them into one. In the Northwest, we sometimes see yellow-shafted Flickers instead of red. To make things more confusing, the two types can mate and create hybrids, or intergrade birds, that have features of both!

PIWO

Pileated Woodpecker

FIELD MARKS

- Red crest
- Black-and-white–striped face
- Heavy, pointed bill

Dryocopus pileatus

HABITAT
Forests with dead and decaying wood

DIET
Carpenter ants, beetles, termites, and other insects; also fruits and nuts

NEST
Giant excavated cavity with a rectangular opening, lined with wood chips

CALLS & SONGS
Calls include a loud *wik-wik-wik-wik*; drum is low and slow

RANGE

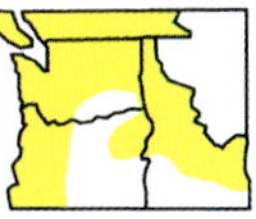

SIZE M

Length ~16"
Wingspan ~29"

This huge woodpecker has a black body, a black-and-white–striped face, and a bright red crest. Almost the size of a crow, the Pileated (PILL-ee-ay-tid or PIE-lee-ay-tid) Woodpecker is the largest woodpecker in the Pacific Northwest and is usually found in older forests with large trees. On a hike, you may hear its loud drumming or the distinct *wik-wik-wik-wik* calls it makes while flapping through the forest. Even if it's not making a racket, you'll know that a Pileated Woodpecker is around if you find large rectangles excavated in the trunks of trees. They make these holes while hunting for ants.

DID YOU KNOW?

Woodpeckers have extremely long tongues that they use to reach into tree cavities and grab insects. How do they fit such a long tongue inside their relatively small head? A woodpecker's tongue actually wraps around the back of its brain when it's not out lapping up bugs! Having a tongue wrapped around its brain makes sense, because when a woodpecker drums its head against the trunk of a tree, its tongue may help protect its brain!

Other Woodpeckers

Woodpeckers have stiff tails that they use to prop themselves up on the sides of trees. They use their thick, pointy bills to peel bark or to dig out wood to uncover insects. Woodpeckers nest in tree cavities that they excavate. They're usually found alone or in pairs. Depending on where you live in the Pacific Northwest, you might see or hear a few other woodpeckers when you're out birding.

AMERICAN THREE-TOED WOODPECKER

Black with some white feathers mixed in; can be hard to find and prefers recently burned forests

BLACK-BACKED WOODPECKER

Completely black back blends in perfectly with charred bark of burnt trees in preferred habitat; males and young birds have yellow crowns

WHITE-HEADED WOODPECKER

Best identified by its white head, with a red patch in back on males; prefers forests with lots of ponderosa pines

LEWIS'S WOODPECKER (BNFB)

Striking bird with iridescent green head and back, reddish face, gray collar, and pink breast, often catches insects from a perch and flies like a crow in a straight path with slow flaps instead of bobbing up and down like other woodpeckers

FALCONS & FLYCATCHERS

Falcons are birds of prey, but they're probably more closely related to parrots than to the other raptors! Falcons are known for killing their prey with their sharp beaks, not with their talons like hawks, eagles, and owls.

Flycatchers, as you might have guessed, catch flies. They're known for perching in one spot and flying out to catch flies and other insects from the air before returning to their perch. This behavior is called sallying. Some fly-catchers are colorful with field marks that can be seen from a distance, while others are plain looking and can be tough to identify, since many look alike.

AMKE

American Kestrel

Falco sparverius

FIELD MARKS

- Two dark face stripes
- Bluish wings and crown
- Rust-colored back
- Dark spots

HABITAT
Open areas

DIET
Rodents, small mammals, reptiles, insects, and small birds

NEST
In cavities made by woodpeckers, openings in buildings

CALLS & SONGS
Rapid, high-pitched *ki-ki-ki-ki*

RANGE

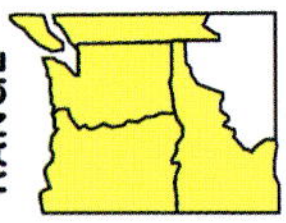

SIZE

M

Length ~10"
Wingspan ~22"

The tiniest and most colorful falcon in North America, the American Kestrel is easy to spot on power lines along roads once you know what to look for. In open areas, you'll see this round little raptor perched on a wire, post, or fence, pumping its tail up and down. If you stay and watch a while, you might see it fly out over a field and hover in place, sometimes quite high above the ground. Once it spots a rodent or other small animal below, it will drop onto its prey and then carry it back to a perch to eat. Unlike most birds of prey, male and female kestrels look quite different from one another. The male has blue shoulders, a blue crown, a reddish tail, and black spots on its back and belly. The female is reddish brown with a tan crown and brown streaks on her belly. Both have two black stripes on both sides of their face.

American Kestrel hunting

DID YOU KNOW?

Unlike humans, birds can see ultraviolet light, so they see the world in a very different way. Birds like American Kestrels can see urine, which glows in ultraviolet light, from a great distance, including the urine of their favorite food: voles. When they hover over a field, kestrels see trails of vole urine like lines in the grass, leading them right to their next meal.

MERLIN

A look-alike falcon that is often confused with the American Kestrel. A bit stockier and darker overall than a kestrel, the Merlin has a pale eyebrow. Merlins don't usually hover like kestrels, and they hunt their prey more like a Peregrine Falcon does, with fast-paced chases.

PEFA

Peregrine Falcon

Falco peregrinus

FIELD MARKS

- Dark hood and mustache
- Pointed wings
- Sharp, hooked bill
- Sharp talons

HABITAT
Coastal cliffs, mountains, canyons, wetlands, and cities

DIET
More than 450 species of birds

NEST
Scrape in the sand or gravel on a cliff, ledge, or human-made structure

CALLS & SONGS
Series of harsh, scratchy *kek-kek-kek* notes

RANGE

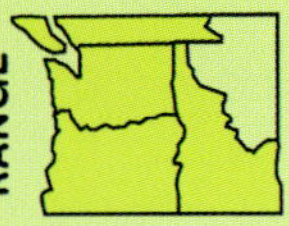

SIZE M

Length ~17"
Wingspan ~40"

These falcons are known for their speed. In fact, Peregrine Falcons are the fastest animals on the planet! They will drop onto other birds from above in an incredible controlled dive called a stoop, reaching speeds of more than 200 miles per hour. They stun or kill their prey with their powerful talons or by biting the animal's neck before carrying it off. Peregrines usually nest on cliffs but have adapted to live in cities, where they nest on bridges and tall buildings. In fact, Peregrine Falcons live in downtown Portland, Seattle, Boise, and Vancouver, BC. In the countryside, these birds hunt songbirds, gamebirds, shorebirds, and ducks. In the city, they hunt pigeons and starlings.

PRAIRIE FALCON

Lives in drier environments and is smaller than the Peregrine Falcon. It is brown overall and has a pale belly with lots of dark markings.

WEKI

Western Kingbird

Tyrannus verticalis

FIELD MARKS

- Gray head and back
- Yellow belly
- Black tail with white edges

HABITAT
Open areas, sometimes near forest edges

DIET
Mostly insects

NEST
Cup of sticks, lined with soft materials, in trees or on power poles or buildings

CALLS & SONGS
Sharp *whit* calls and sounds like squeaky toys

RANGE

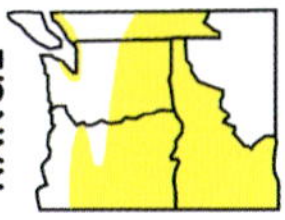

SIZE

Length ~9"
Wingspan ~15"

This large flycatcher is gray above and yellow below. In flight, it flashes its black tail with white outer tail feathers. You'll find Western Kingbirds perched in the open on telephone wires, fences, or trees. They fly out to catch insects and often return to the same perch. This bird is aggressive near its nest and will snap its bill and dive-bomb people and predators who get too close—even hawks and kestrels. It will also raise its crown of bright red feathers that it usually keeps hidden under the gray feathers on its head.

EASTERN KINGBIRD

Black above and white below with a white-tipped tail. They may not look like their Western Kingbird cousins, but they share many of the same behaviors.

TROPICAL KINGBIRD

Usually found only along the coast in the Pacific Northwest. They look like Western Kingbirds but are larger, with thicker bills. They have more yellow on their chest and don't have white outer tail feathers.

WEWP

Western Wood-Pewee

Contopus sordidulus

FIELD MARKS

- Plain gray above
- No wing bars or eye ring
- Pale belly

HABITAT
Forests and open areas

DIET
Mostly flying insects

NEST
Cup made of plant materials and spiderwebs, lined with grass and feathers

CALLS & SONGS
Buzzy, whistled *pee-wee!*

RANGE

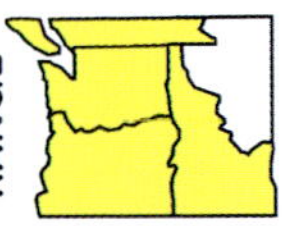

SIZE

S

Length ~6"
Wingspan ~10"

Flycatchers can look so much alike that even expert birders struggle to identify them. But it helps to know a bird's facial markings; tail, wing, and beak length; calls; and movements. If there's one plain-looking flycatcher that you should learn to identify, it's the Western Wood-Pewee. This common bird's song includes a buzzy, whistled *pee-wee!* When you hear it in spring or summer, look for a dark, slim bird with a pale belly, usually flying out from a perch to catch insects. This bird is known to leave its perch to catch an insect in flight and then return to the same perch, over and over again.

DID YOU KNOW?

Like the Western Bluebird and the Western Meadowlark, the Western Wood-Pewee has an eastern counterpart—and in this case, it's a nearly identical bird. Even though the Eastern Wood-Pewee looks almost exactly like the Western Wood-Pewee, the two birds don't live in the same place and their songs are very different.

SAPH

Say's Phoebe

(BNFB)

Sayornis saya

FIELD MARKS
- Peaked crown
- Pinkish orange belly and undertail
- Grayish brown back
- Dark tail

HABITAT
Dry, open areas

DIET
Insects caught in the air or on the ground

NEST
Cup of plant material and rocks, lined with feathers and hair, tucked in protected area

CALLS & SONGS
Clear, sad *whee-err* whistle that slurs downward; quick hiccup sound

RANGE

SIZE

S

Length ~7"
Wingspan ~13"

This flycatcher has a grayish brown back and a pinkish orange belly and undertail. Like other flycatchers, it hunts insects from perches and is often found along fences. The Say's Phoebe is quite hardy and breeds farther north than any other flycatcher. You'll find them in drier open areas in the eastern parts of the Northwest, and not usually near forests or waterways. They're known to nest almost anywhere, including in barns, on old machines, in mailboxes, and in the old nests of other birds!

BLACK PHOEBE

This flycatcher is black with a white belly and often hunts from low perches over water. They may nest close to people in old buildings or barns and under bridges. They are expanding their range north and are becoming more common in the Pacific Northwest.

ASH-THROATED FLYCATCHER

Large, long-tailed birds that live in dry, open country. They don't typically catch flies like their cousins. Instead, they grab insects from trees, bushes, or the ground.

Other Flycatchers

Flycatchers are known for flying out from their perches to catch insects on the wing. But they're also known for hawking, where they hover in midair and pick insects off leaves. Some flycatchers are brightly colored and easy to identify in the field, while others look alike and can be difficult to identify, even with a clear view or photograph. A few flycatchers look so similar that they can be identified only by their calls, and a silent bird cannot always be confidently identified.

OLIVE-SIDED FLYCATCHER

Large flycatcher with a dark "vest" on its breast, a white throat, and a distinct whistled song that sounds like *quick, three cheers*; usually hunts flying insects from a perch atop a tall tree

WILLOW FLYCATCHER

Similar to Western Wood-Pewee in size and shape, but paler with much shorter wings, and it sings an easy-to-learn, hoarse *fitz-bew!* song

WESTERN FLYCATCHER

Yellowish belly, teardrop-shaped white eye ring, and a *see-yeet* call that sounds like someone whistling to get your attention; once considered two separate species: Pacific-slope Flycatcher and Cordilleran Flycatcher

HAMMOND'S FLYCATCHER

Hammond's, Gray, and Dusky Flycatchers are difficult to tell apart. Birders must look for a combination of specific field marks while listening closely for songs and call notes. Hammond's have longer looking wings and a shorter looking tail. They also sit with more upright posture.

GRAY FLYCATCHER

Similar to Hammond's and Dusky, but paler, and tends to wag its tail downwards; also prefers open, drier habitat

DUSKY FLYCATCHER

Similar to Hammond's and Gray, with shorter looking wings, longer looking tail; tends to flick its tail upwards

SHRIKES & VIREOS

Shrikes are songbirds that act like raptors. These little hunters have sharp, hooked beaks and are known for capturing small animals and then storing them on thorns or barbed-wire fences to eat later. They're usually seen perched out in the open, waiting to swoop down on their next meal. **Vireos are smaller songbirds** that also have hooked beaks. They're also considered predatory, but they hunt mostly insects and eat fruits. They're sometimes confused for warblers, but they're usually thicker looking and slower moving, and they have that hooked beak.

WAVI

Warbling Vireo

Vireo gilvus

FIELD MARKS

- Plain looking
- Pale eyebrow
- Dark line through eye
- Thick bill

HABITAT
Deciduous forests, neighborhoods, and parks

DIET
Insects, spiders, and sometimes berries

NEST
Cup of plant material, hair, and lichen, hanging under a branch

CALLS & SONGS
Fast series of whistles and warbles that rise and fall

RANGE

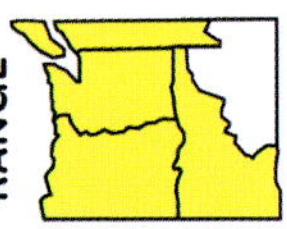

SIZE

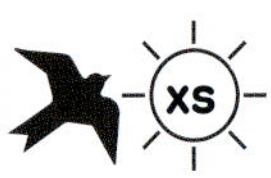

Length ~5"
Wingspan ~9"

This small, plain-looking bird is difficult to see, but it's easy to listen for if you know its song. In spring and summer, you may hear this bird's rich, musical song on almost any walk. The song is a fast series of whistles and warbles that rise and fall. Follow the sound and look for a small grayish bird with a light-colored belly and a pale eyebrow. It's often seen hunting insects in the leaves of a tree or shrub alongside warblers, kinglets, or nut-hatches, but it tends to move much slower than these other birds. If you manage a good look, you'll notice that the Warbling Vireo stands out among the warblers and kinglets due to its thick, straight bill with a tiny hook at the end. Depending on where you live, a Warbling Vireo can look and sound quite differ-ent. Scientists have named half a dozen subspecies that vary quite a bit in size, coloring, and song patterns.

HUTTON'S VIREO (BNFB)

Looks a lot like the Ruby-crowned Kinglet, but it has a thicker bill with a sharply hooked tip, and it moves much slower than a kinglet. These birds sing *zu-wee* and *zo-zoo* songs on repeat for minutes on end.

CASSIN'S VIREO (BNFB)

Olive-green above, with a blue-gray head, a thick bill, and a wide white eye ring.

RED-EYED VIREO

Has red eyes, of course, and pale eyebrows outlined in black. It sings a nonstop song that sounds like it's asking a question and then answering it, over and over.

NSHR

Northern Shrike

Lanius borealis

FIELD MARKS
- Dark mask
- Thick bill with hooked tip
- Pale gray back
- Black wings and tail

HABITAT
Open areas with brushy cover

DIET
Insects, birds, lizards, and small mammals

NEST
Deep cup of twigs filled and lined with feathers, moss, and animal hair

CALLS & SONGS
Call is a harsh *shack!*; sings low warbles and squeaky notes

RANGE

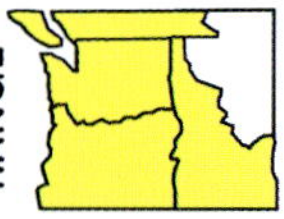

SIZE S

Length ~10"
Wingspan ~14"

Shrikes are unusual songbirds that hunt and eat insects, lizards, rodents, and even other birds! They are gray and black, with a blocky head, black mask, and thick bill with a small, sharply hooked tip. If you spot a Northern Shrike perched on a fence or in a shrub, stick around to watch it hunt. Because they're songbirds and don't have talons like birds of prey, they use their sharp, hooked bill to kill prey. And they often store their catch for later by impaling it on a thorn or a barbed-wire fence. This habit of stabbing and hanging up their food gives them a very memorable nickname, "butcher birds."

LOGGERHEAD SHRIKE

Similar looking but slightly smaller, with a cleaner white belly and a much thicker black mask with less white markings.

CORVIDS

Crows, ravens, jays, nutcrackers, and magpies are all corvids. These large songbirds have sharp, strong bills. They're known for being quite loud and highly intelligent. They can be mischievous and playful. Most corvids are social, and some of them travel in large flocks. Most are omnivores, meaning they eat a wide variety of things including seeds, nuts, fruits, insects, and other small animals including other birds.

STJA

Steller's Jay (BNFB)

Cyanocitta stelleri

FIELD MARKS

- Shaggy, black crest
- Bluish forehead marks
- Blue wings and tail

HABITAT	DIET	NEST	CALLS & SONGS
Evergreen forests and mixed forests, neighborhoods, and parks	Insects, seeds, berries, nuts, small animals, and other birds' eggs and nestlings	Cup of twigs and leaves lined with grass, high in a tree	Harsh, loud, and fast *shack-shack-shack* and long, piercing *chaaak!*

RANGE

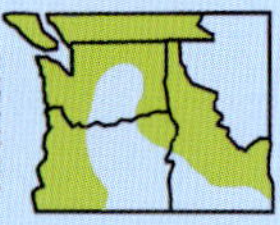

SIZE M

Length ~12"
Wingspan ~19"

This bird is blue and it's a jay, but it's not a Blue Jay. The Steller's Jay is a large, dark blue jay with a black head and a shaggy mohawk. Like many members of the jay family, it is bold, curious, and loud. You'll often hear this bird screaming before it swoops into view. They also whistle, rattle, and gurgle, and they can even impersonate other birds. They do a nearly perfect impression of a Red-tailed Hawk's cry, and this impersonation can scare other birds away from a backyard feeder! They like to eat peanuts and suet and will even learn to beg humans for food. Some act like thieves and steal food from picnickers in parks and campgrounds. Many jays are nest robbers, and Steller's Jays are no different. They often raid other birds' nests and eat their eggs or chicks. Sometimes they will even attack and eat smaller adult birds!

DID YOU KNOW?

Jays are smart birds! Groups of Steller's Jays will sometimes have a sentry bird that acts as a lookout while the others forage for food in the forest. They also plan ahead! Steller's Jays will stash multiple seeds or nuts in their bills and then bury or hide them, one by one. When winter approaches and food is harder to find, they remember these hiding spots and retrieve their stashed food.

CALIFORNIA SCRUB-JAY

Don't just live in California. These blue jays are common in the Pacific Northwest too, but they have gray bellies and don't have a crest.

CANADA JAY

Very different from the Steller's Jay and the California Scrub-Jay. These smaller jays are gray and white and can be overly friendly. They often eat right from people's hands! They tend to live in the deep forest and travel in small groups.

Black-billed Magpie

Pica hudsonia

FIELD MARKS

- Long, dark tail
- White wing patch
- Blue and black feathers
- Black bill

HABITAT
Farm country and open ranch-land, towns, and city parks

DIET
Fruits, seeds, insects, small mammals, carrion, and more

NEST
Large stick nest, usually in a tree, with a grass-lined mud cup inside

CALLS & SONGS
Loud, harsh *yawk, yawk, yawk* and thin, high-pitched *yeer*

RANGE

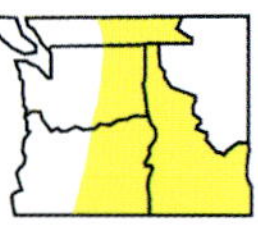

SIZE L

Length ~20"
Wingspan ~24"

This long-tailed, iridescent black-and-white bird is common in the drier eastern parts of the Northwest. Like their cousins the ravens, crows, and jays, Black-billed Magpies are intelligent and noisy. This makes magpies easy to find—they're not the kind of bird you need to search around for in thick brush or steal a look at from a great distance. They're usually spotted out in the open, feeding on roadkill, perched on a fencepost, or flashing their white wing patches as they fly across an open area. In some parts of the Northwest, they even visit back-yard feeders. Magpies often travel in groups, and if you're out birding, especially near a river, you'll probably hear them before you see them.

DID YOU KNOW?

Black-billed Magpies are sometimes spotted around or perched atop larger mammals like deer and cattle. That's because they like to pick ticks and other insects off these animals' skin. This helps both animals, as the mammal gets nasty pests removed from its skin and the Magpie gets an easy meal.

CLARK'S NUTCRACKER

Large, gray members of the corvid family, with large black bills and black wings with white patches. They live in conifer forests and are known to collect and store pine seeds for the winter.

PINYON JAY

Grayish blue with long black bills, and they live in dry pine and juniper forests. They tend to wander over large areas and sometimes congregate in large, noisy flocks.

AMCR

American Crow

Corvus brachyrhynchos

FIELD MARKS

- Long, heavy bill
- Fan-shaped tail in flight
- Black plumage

HABITAT
Various habitats; prefers cities, towns, and farmland

DIET
Grains, fruit, nuts, small invertebrates, mammals and birds, eggs, carrion, and trash

NEST
Twig nest with an inner cup of pine needles, bark, and hair

CALLS & SONGS
Classic *caw*, rattles, clicks, and coos

RANGE

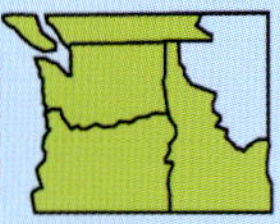

SIZE

Length ~19"
Wingspan ~38"

These birds are so familiar and entertaining that even non-birders tend to notice and enjoy watching them! The American Crow is a large, dark, highly intelligent corvid. There's a lot to admire about these birds: They build and use simple tools and can solve puzzles. They live in large and complicated family groups. And they have incredible memories—they can even remember people's faces! While most of us enjoy watching their antics, some people are bothered by their noise and the messes they make, especially in winter when they form large groups. Some winter roosts have been around for years and attract hundreds—or even thousands—of birds every night. Whether you love them or hate them, crows are here to stay. These clever and adaptable birds are happy to live in our towns and cities.

DID YOU KNOW?

Crows are known to hold "funerals" for family members and friends. It's something ornithologists have been studying and trying to understand for a long time. When a crow dies, other crows gather near the bird and call loudly. After gathering and making a lot of noise, the birds leave the scene. Some scientists think crows hold these funerals to see what may have killed one of their own and to learn more about potential dangers.

COMMON RAVEN

People often confuse American Crows with their much larger, more solitary cousin. But ravens tend to form smaller groups and live in more rural settings. They have shaggy feathers on their throat, a larger and curvier bill, and a wide, wedge-shaped tail that's visible in flight. If you listen closely, you'll notice that crows *caw* while ravens tend to croak!

OTHER SONGBIRDS

A lot of birds are considered songbirds—even crows and ravens. But the birds covered here are all smaller perching birds and are loosely related. These songbirds include **chickadees, larks, swallows, kinglets, nuthatches, creepers, sparrows, finches, warblers, tanagers, buntings, and grosbeaks**. Some of these birds are in the Pacific Northwest year round, and others migrate and are here only during the warmer months of the year.

Songbirds are sometimes called perching birds, since their toes are arranged in a way that helps them grab onto and perch on branches. They're also called passerines (PASS-err-inz or PASS-err-eenz) because they all belong to a larger group (or order) of birds known by the Latin name Passeriformes. More than half of all bird species on the planet belong to this order, and many have a special vocal organ called a syrinx that helps them sing their complex songs.

BCCH

Black-capped Chickadee

Poecile atricapillus

HABITAT
Mixed forests and parks

DIET
Seeds, fruit, insects, and spiders

NEST
Cup of moss and plant material inside a tree cavity or nest box

CALLS & SONGS
Chicka-dee-dee calls; whistled *fee-bee* song

RANGE

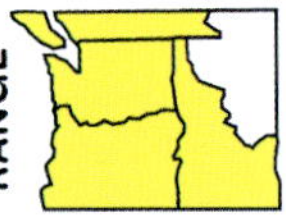

SIZE

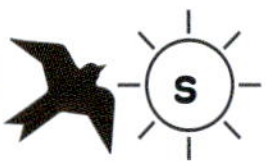

Length ~5"
Wingspan ~7"

This cute little bird is so familiar that many people know its name even before they become birders. The most common chickadee throughout the Pacific Northwest, the Black-capped Chickadee has a big round head and almost no neck. Regular visitors to many backyard bird feeders, these black-and-white birds can be seen and heard in a wide variety of habitats. Many people know their famous *chicka-dee-dee* calls as well as their clear *fee-bee* whistled songs. When you hear these calls or songs, look for a little bird hopping in the branches of a tree or hanging upside down from a twig as it reaches out for something to eat. In winter, they often join mixed flocks with kinglets, nuthatches, Downy Woodpeckers, and other birds, all working together to find food and avoid predators.

FIELD MARKS
- Short bill
- Black throat and cap
- White cheek

DID YOU KNOW?

The chickadee's famous *chicka-dee-dee-dee* call can communicate information to other birds about nearby predators. When a chickadee adds more *dee* notes to the end of the call, it means a bigger threat or a more dangerous predator is close. A person walking by a chickadee might be greeted with a *chicka-dee-dee-dee*, while a hunting Cooper's Hawk or a roosting owl might cause this bird to make a very long and loud *chicka-dee-dee-dee-dee-dee-dee!*

MOUNTAIN CHICKADEE

Has white eyebrows, and its calls are harsher and angrier sounding.

Has a rich brown back and is smaller than the Black-capped Chickadee. Its *chicka-dee-dee-dee* call sounds like a squeaky toy.

CHESTNUT-BACKED CHICKADEE

PUMA

Purple Martin

Progne subis

HABITAT	DIET	NEST	CALLS & SONGS
Open areas, forests, and near water	Flying insects	Twig and mud nest in a hole in a tree, building, or birdhouse	Calls include *zeet* and *zhee-hee*; song is a loud jumble of chirps and rattles

RANGE

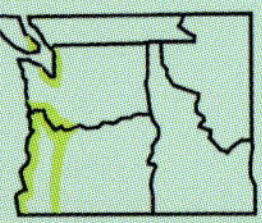

SIZE S

Length ~8"
Wingspan ~16"

Our largest species of swallow lives in groups that often nest in specially made birdhouses. Though Purple Martins once lived in cavities in trees, Indigenous people in North America started hanging hollowed-out gourds near their homes, and the Purple Martins moved in. Many people still hang up gourd-style houses and "condominium" birdhouses for Purple Martins. They make good neighbors and help control mosquitoes. Males are a shiny bluish purple but can look almost black. Females are dark grayish blue above and pale underneath. In open areas in summer, listen for their friendly-sounding chirps and rattles and look for these large, dark birds swooping through the air.

FIELD MARKS

- Hooked bill
- Forked tail
- Male: dark bluish purple plumage
- Female: dull gray with dark and bluish parts

MALE

FEMALE

DID YOU KNOW?

Like other swallows, Purple Martins don't just eat on the wing—they drink while flying too! The next time you're watching a Purple Martin or another swallow species hunt over water, pay close attention, and you might see it swoop down and skim the surface, scooping up a beak full of water.

BARS

Barn Swallow

Hirundo rustica

FIELD MARKS

- Long, forked tail
- Long wings
- Blue back
- Orange throat, forehead, and belly

HABITAT
Open areas with good nest sites and mud to make nests with

DIET
Flies and other insects

NEST
Cup of mud lined with grass and feathers, in the eaves of a structure or under a bridge

CALLS & SONGS
Calls include a high *kwip*; song is a long series of squeaks and mechanical chirps and whirrs

RANGE

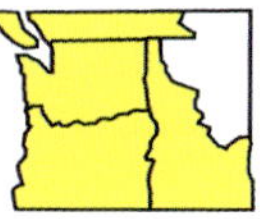

SIZE

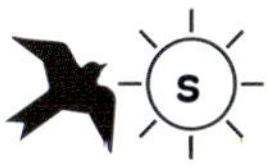

Length ~7"
Wingspan ~12"

This common swallow is dark blue above and pale below with a reddish orange throat and forehead. The Barn Swallow's long, forked tail can help you identify it from far away and compare it to other swallows you may see. These birds can form large groups, often mixed with other swallows, swooping over open areas and sometimes very close to the ground or water. They eat flying insects in summer and seem to spend the whole day catching bugs and bringing them back to their nestlings. You might find one of their amazing mud nests tucked under cover in a barn or shed, or under a bridge.

DID YOU KNOW?

Barn Swallows used to nest mostly in caves, but nowadays they usually nest on human-made structures like barns. In rural areas, it seems like almost every barn, shed, or outbuilding has some swallows nesting in or on it.

Other Swallows

Swallows have very short legs and long, pointy wings. They're known for their acrobatic flight style. They zigzag through the air as they hunt for flying insects. They can be fun to watch, but they can also be hard to identify because they fly so quickly overhead. With each species, try to pick out one special field mark to look for. For example, with a Tree Swallow, look at the amount of white on its face and how its dark eyes are hidden under a dark cap. Compare that to the amount of white on a Violet-green Swallow's face, and notice that its eyes are surrounded by white feathers and stand out much more than those of the Tree Swallow.

TREE SWALLOW

Very common swallow is iridescent blue and black above; dark color extends below the eyes

VIOLET-GREEN SWALLOW

Iridescent green on top, sometimes with hints of purple; the white on its underside extends up around its eyes

NORTHERN ROUGH-WINGED SWALLOW

Light brown above with a pale throat and belly, often seen flying low and catching insects over water

BANK SWALLOW

Smallest swallow in our area is brown above and pale below with a brown band across the breast; nests in burrow on riverbanks

CLIFF SWALLOW

Blue back and crown, chestnut-colored face, and pale forehead patch; colonies of swallows build incredible, almost sphere-shaped mud nests along cliffs, under bridges, and on buildings

HOLA

Horned Lark

Eremophila alpestris

FIELD MARKS

- Black mask and bib
- Black forehead stripe and tiny "horns"
- White outer tail feathers

HABITAT
Bare, open areas with little vegetation—beaches, deserts, plowed fields, and airports

DIET
Seeds and insects

NEST
Small depression in the ground, lined with plant material

CALLS & SONGS
Calls are high chip notes; song is a series of high-pitched, tinkling notes

RANGE

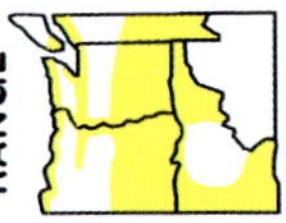

SIZE

Length ~7"
Wingspan ~12"

A true "birder's bird," the Horned Lark is pretty common in certain habitats, but someone who's not very interested in birds could easily overlook it. These small larks blend in well with their surroundings, and they're not always easy to find and see up close. If you do get a clear view, you'll see its beautiful black mask on its white-and-yellow face and a thick, black forehead stripe that lifts into tiny "horns" on the back of its head. The horns are actually little tufts of feathers. These birds are usually seen foraging on the ground or flitting along, singing their high-pitched, tinkling song.

DID YOU KNOW?

A special subspecies of Horned Lark in Oregon and Washington is called the Streaked Horned Lark. It's often much brighter yellow than those found farther inland. As with other grassland species, Streaked Horned Larks populations have been in decline mostly because of habitat loss. Fewer than 2,000 Streaked Horned Larks still live in the Northwest, and many organizations are hard at work tracking them and working to protect them.

BUSH

Bushtit

Psaltriparus minimus

FIELD MARKS

- Sphere shaped
- Short, stubby bill
- Long tail
- Thin legs

HABITAT
Open and wooded areas, parks, and towns

DIET
Mostly insects and spiders

NEST
Sock-shaped hanging nest of plant material and spiderwebs

CALLS & SONGS
High-pitched twittering

RANGE

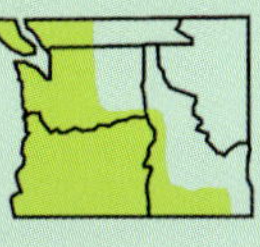

SIZE XS

Length ~4"
Wingspan ~6"

Perched on a branch, a Bushtit looks like a tiny, fluffy gray sphere on stick legs. In flight, these little birds seem to bounce along, one after another, before crowding around a backyard suet feeder, twittering and chirping the whole time. If they visit your feeder, you may be able to get close enough to see their eyes. Females have light-colored eyes and males have dark eyes! In winter, they travel in large flocks. But in summer, pairs of birds, sometimes with helpers, work together to build a unique, sock-shaped hanging nest made of plants and spiderwebs. When the nest is in use, the pair and any helpers sleep inside.

WRENTIT

Live along the Oregon coast. Even though they look a bit like Bushtits and have a similar name, the two birds are not closely related. The Wrentit is very secretive and can be tough to see. It's often heard near the beach, singing a loud series of *dit* notes that speed up at the end like a bouncing ball.

RCKI

Ruby-crowned Kinglet

Corthylio calendula

FIELD MARKS
- White ring around eye
- White wing bars
- Male: ruby crown patch (not always visible)

HABITAT
Mixed forests

DIET
Mostly insects and spiders

NEST
Large sphere of plant material, moss, and spiderwebs, lined with grass and fur

CALLS & SONGS
Harsh, scolding *jit-jit!* calls; songs are high whistles followed by descending notes and warbles

RANGE

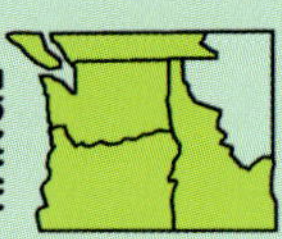

SIZE XS

Length ~4"
Wingspan ~7"

This tiny forest bird never seems to stop moving as it flicks its wings and forages for insects. Seemingly small and plain, it's full of big surprises. It sings an incredibly loud and complicated song. And when it's agitated, you'll understand how it got its name. The male has a patch of bright pink feathers on top of its head that it keeps hidden most of the time. But when it's feeling excited or upset, these feathers rise up to form a neon pink mohawk!

GOLDEN-CROWNED KINGLET

A bit smaller than its ruby-crowned cousin. Tends to stay high in the trees and is harder to spot. It has a neon-yellow-orange stripe that it raises up when it's excited.

HUTTON'S VIREO (BNFB)

Looks a lot like a Ruby-crowned Kinglet but not related. Chunkier, with a thicker bill and a wider white eye ring, and doesn't have a secret pink mohawk.

CEDW

Cedar Waxwing

Bombycilla cedrorum

FIELD MARKS
- Black mask
- Shaggy, pointed crest
- Red, waxy wingtips
- Yellow-tipped tail

HABITAT
Almost anywhere with berries

DIET
Fruit, mostly berries, and some insects

NEST
Large woven cup of plant material, string, horsehair, and more, lined with grass and pine needles

CALLS & SONGS
Soft, high-pitched, whistled *zeeee*

RANGE

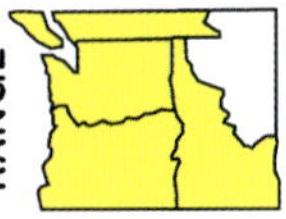

SIZE S

Length ~8"
Wingspan ~12"

This unusual-looking bird is named for the red, waxy tips on some of its feathers and for its love of cedar berries. It has a slicked-back, pointy crest and a striking black mask. It's brownish overall with a yellow belly and a square tail that looks like it was dipped in bright yellow paint. These birds love fruit, and flocks are often seen devouring berries from a shrub or tree. They are incredibly entertaining to watch as they eat. After a while you might see them passing berries back and forth with flock mates or tossing berries into the air before eating them. Listen for their high-pitched whistle calls when they fly overhead.

BOHEMIAN WAXWING

Visits parts of the Pacific Northwest, but only in winter. They look like Cedar Waxwings but have a gray belly and a cinnamon-colored patch under the tail.

RBNU

Red-breasted Nuthatch

Sitta canadensis

FIELD MARKS
- White eyebrow
- Black cap and eye line
- Reddish breast and belly

HABITAT
Evergreen forests

DIET
Insects in spring and summer; seeds in fall and winter

NEST
Tree cavity lined with grass, pine needles, feathers, and bark

CALLS & SONGS
High-pitched, nasal *yank* that sounds like a little horn

RANGE

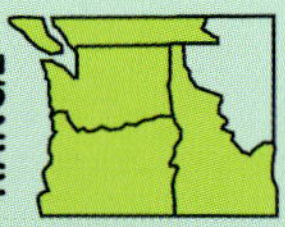

SIZE

Length ~5"
Wingspan ~8"

This tiny, hyperactive songbird is known for spending time walking upside down on tree trunks or briefly appearing at feeders to grab a single seed before flying off. The Red-breasted Nuthatch is a compact little bird with almost no neck. Its back is bluish gray and its breast and belly are reddish colored. It has a thin and slightly upturned bill, a short tail, and a boldly patterned face. Look closely and you'll see a black cap, a white eyebrow, and a thick black stripe that runs through its eye. In spring and summer, these birds are seen traveling up and down tree trunks, searching for insects. In fall and winter, they're busy collecting seeds and nuts and wedging them into the bark of trees. They hammer food into the bark with their bills to store it there and eat it later.

DID YOU KNOW?

Red-breasted Nuthatches sometimes excavate their own nest cavities, and sometimes they take over other birds' old nest sites. When they're busy lining a nest cavity with soft and dry materials, they might even steal some from the nests of other birds! They also collect sticky resin from trees and spread it around the entrance to their nest cavity, which may help to disguise the nest hole and keep predators from finding their nestlings. Sometimes they use a small piece of bark as a tool to apply the resin.

WHITE-BREASTED NUTHATCH

Much larger than the Red-breasted Nuthatch and has a white breast instead of a reddish one. It also has a black hood and a clean white face without a black eye line.

PYGMY NUTHATCH

A bit smaller than Red-breasted Nuthatches. They have a cream-colored belly and a dark cap that extends down over their eyes, and they tend to live in drier areas where ponderosa pine trees grow.

BRCR

Brown Creeper

Certhia americana

FIELD MARKS
- Thin, downcurved bill
- Streaky brown back
- White throat and belly

HABITAT
Mixed forests

DIET
Insects and spiders

NEST
Hammock-shaped nest tucked behind flaps of loose tree bark

CALLS & SONGS
Call is a high, warbly *tsee*; song sounds like *trees, trees, beautiful trees!*

RANGE

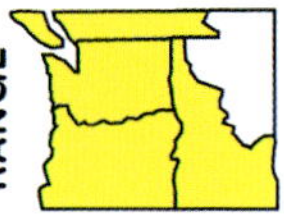

SIZE XS

Length ~5"
Wingspan ~7"

This unusual songbird is like a miniature brown woodpecker, clinging to the side of a tree and supported by a long, stiff tail. It spirals up a tree trunk, probing for insects in the furrows of the bark along the way. When it gets near the top, it dives down to the base of a neighboring tree and spirals up again. The colors in its streaky brown back blend in with the tree bark. Once you learn to recognize its distinct call (a high, warbly *tsee*) and its unusual song (like a high-pitched *trees, trees, beautiful trees!*), you'll have a better chance of finding one creeping up a tree trunk on your next bird walk.

DID YOU KNOW?

Brown Creepers build nests in two separate parts: a hammock-shaped frame made of twigs and bark with a small cup inside that's made of soft materials like moss, grass, feathers, and hair. The nest is on the side of a tree, behind a flap of loose bark! Creepers use the sticky cocoons and egg cases of insects to glue the pieces together and attach them to the bark flap.

PAWR

Pacific Wren

Troglodytes pacificus

FIELD MARKS
- Short, narrow tail
- Pale eyebrow
- Dark barring on belly, wings, and tail

HABITAT
Mixed forests

DIET
Insects

NEST
Dome of moss, twigs, bark, and other plant material, lined with hair and feathers

CALLS & SONGS
Long song with dozens of trills, chirps, and buzzes

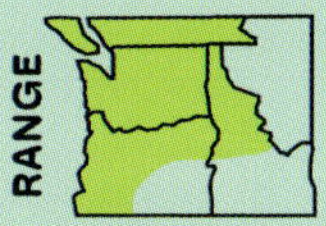

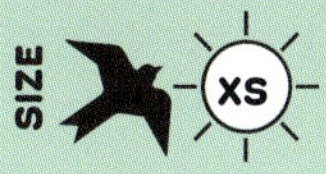

Length ~4"
Wingspan ~5"

This is a great example of a tiny bird with a huge voice! The Pacific Wren's song can last more than ten seconds and is made up of as many as 50 different trills, chirps, and buzzes. It's a long and loud song, especially coming from such a small, round bird. It has a short tail and wings and can look almost spherical. It tends to stay low in the forest, flying short distances and hopping over the ground. During the breeding season, males will pop on a branch or find a low perch and belt out impressive songs. Otherwise, it can be hard to spot this tiny brown bird scurrying through ferns and thick vegetation.

DID YOU KNOW?
Some other bird species are remarkably similar to the Pacific Wren. In fact, up until 2010, they were all assumed to be the same species. Scientists changed their thinking, however, and now consider the Pacific Wren a separate species from the very similar Winter Wren of eastern North America and the Eurasian Wren from Europe.

BEWR

Bewick's Wren (BNFB)

Thryomanes bewickii

FIELD MARKS

- Pale belly
- White eyebrow
- Brown upperparts
- Long, barred tail

HABITAT
Brushy areas

DIET
Insects and other small invertebrates

NEST
Cup of sticks, leaves, and other plant material, lined with snake-skin and other soft things

CALLS & SONGS
Short song begins with clear notes, then buzzy phrases, and finally a trill

RANGE

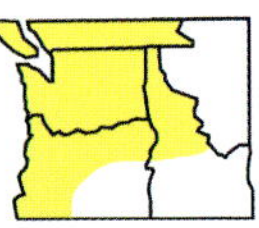

SIZE XS

Length ~5"
Wingspan ~7"

This wren is notoriously loud and aggressive for a small, plain-looking bird. The Bewick's Wren has a brown back, a pale belly, and a thick, white eyebrow. Like other wrens, its song is loud and full of trills and whistles and its calls are harsh and angry sounding. Sometimes this bird sneaks through thick brush and can be hard to see clearly. But it may choose a perch out in the open and sing its loud, musical song. These little birds are common, and you may find them living in a nearby park or in your own backyard. Bewick's Wrens are best identified by their white eyebrows and long, barred tails—and by their tendency to be noisy! When a young male wren is growing up, he listens to the songs of his parents and those of adults in neighboring territories. He borrows from the songs he hears and changes a few notes or phrases to make a song of his own.

NORTHERN HOUSE WREN

Everywhere in summer, singing their long, bubbly songs that begin with harsh, scolding calls. This smaller, plainer wren doesn't have pale eyebrows like the Bewick's Wren.

CANYON WREN

Often heard along steep river canyons, where they sing songs that begin with sweet, descending whistles and end with harsh notes.

ROCK WREN

Pale with a long bill and lives in dry, rocky places around the Pacific Northwest.

MARSH WREN

Common in wetlands in summer, where they constantly sing their scratchy, buzzy songs while hidden in thickets or perched in cattails.

SATH

Sage Thrasher

Oreoscoptes montanus

FIELD MARKS
- Short, curved bill
- Streaky undersides
- Long tail

HABITAT
Open areas with sagebrush

DIET
Insects and berries

NEST
Large nest made of twigs, lined with soft plant material and fur

CALLS & SONGS
Calls include harsh scolding and a low *shuck*; song a mixture of trills, warbles, whistles, and impressions of other birds

RANGE

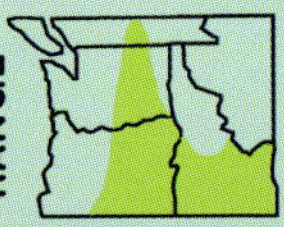

SIZE

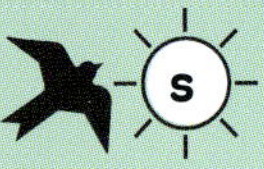

Length ~9"
Wingspan ~12"

Thrashers search for food on the ground by "thrashing" their curved beaks through leaf litter (decomposing leaves) and topsoil. Often hidden under sagebrush, looking for insects and berries, the Sage Thrasher sometimes perches out in the open and sings a long, complicated song. They're known to mimic (copy) the songs of other birds and to sing for minutes on end, sometimes in the middle of the night. Like other thrashers, the Sage Thrasher often runs away from predators on foot instead of flying away. Along with other unique birds, it lives in sage-brush steppe habitat, which is open and mostly flat, with a lot of sagebrush and other low shrubs and grasses. When you're driving through sagebrush steppe it might look like an empty space, but it's really a diverse and important habitat for many species. This habitat is threatened in the Northwest because it's been divided up into small fragments and changed by grazing livestock and by people controlling the natural cycle of wildfires.

NORTHERN MOCKINGBIRD

Another well-known mimic and is found in parts of southern Oregon and southern Idaho. This mostly gray bird has a long tail and white wing patches that it flashes in flight.

GRAY CATBIRD

Lives in eastern Oregon and Washington and in parts of Idaho. You may hear its strange catlike *mew* call or spot the gray bird with a black cap as it moves through thick brush.

EUST

European Starling

Sturnus vulgaris

FIELD MARKS

- Bright yellow bill
- Iridescent, glossy plumage
- Short tail

HABITAT
Near people, almost anywhere

DIET
Insects and invertebrates, fruit, seeds, and trash

NEST
Cup of plant material in a tree cavity or nest box

CALLS & SONGS
Purrs, rattles, shrieks, whistles, chatters, trills, and many other sounds

RANGE

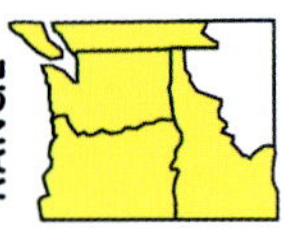

SIZE

S

Length ~9"
Wingspan ~14"

Brought to New York City from Europe more than 100 years ago, European Starlings have now spread across much of North America. They're known for competing with some native birds for nest sites and for forming massive flocks in winter. While many people, even birders, dislike this nonnative bird, it's undeniably beautiful. Adults are speckled silver and glossy black, with iridescent green-and-purple feathers. They make an impressive variety of sounds and can mimic other birds, frogs, cats, goats, human voices, and even some machines!

HOUSE SPARROW

MALE

FEMALE

Even though they're not related, the House Sparrow is often associated with the starling. It's also nonnative and was introduced to North America on purpose in the 1800s, and it has spread to almost everywhere people live across the continent. Like the starling, this sparrow is not always the most popular bird, but when you view it up close, you'll see that it's beautiful and fun to watch!

AMDI

American Dipper

Cinclus mexicanus

HABITAT
Along creeks, streams, and small rivers

DIET
Insects and small aquatic invertebrates

NEST
Dome of moss and leaves with a nest of dry grass inside

CALLS & SONGS
Loud, bubbly song of repeated phrases that can last for several minutes

RANGE

SIZE S

Length ~7"
Wingspan ~11"

North America's aquatic songbird! The American Dipper is a small, dark gray songbird that spends its whole life in the rushing water of streams or rivers. It often perches on a rock, bobbing its body up and down, or dives under the water to catch insects and other invertebrates. Perfectly suited to life in the water, it has oil glands that help waterproof its feathers and flaps on its nostrils that act like nose plugs when it dives. To find an American Dipper near fast-moving water, look for rocks with splatters of white poop. You may see this aquatic bird as it bobs on rocks, flies low over the water, or swims in the rushing current.

DID YOU KNOW?

If you're lucky enough to watch a dipper hunting in a creek or river, you'll probably notice that it seems to blink a lot more than other birds. It's not necessarily blinking more, but with its bright white, feathered eyelids, its blinking is much more noticeable. Most birds have dark eyelids without feathers. Scientists aren't sure why dippers have these unusual and striking eyelids.

FIELD MARKS
- Short tail
- Round body
- Sharp, thin bill
- White-feathered eyelids

WEBL

Western Bluebird

Sialia mexicana

FIELD MARKS

- Blue head and back
- Reddish chest and flanks
- Thin, straight bill

HABITAT
Open areas near forests; also scrubland and high desert

DIET
Insects in summer; fruits and seeds in winter

NEST
Cup of plant material lined with grass, hair, and other soft items in a tree cavity or nest box

CALLS & SONGS
Calls include chattering *chee-chee*; song is series of whistled *pyew* notes

RANGE

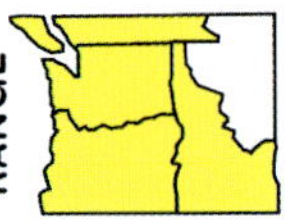

SIZE

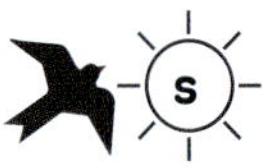

Length ~7"
Wingspan ~12"

This charming blue bird swoops down from low perches to hunt for insects along the ground. Once a more common sight in the Pacific Northwest, it has struggled for many years due to habitat loss, introduced competing species, and an increase in the use of pesticides. They nest in cavities but don't excavate their own. Instead, they use old woodpecker cavities or nest boxes provided by people. Males are bright blue with reddish chests and sides, and females are grayish blue above with hints of orange-brown underneath. If you live in an open area or near farmland, put up a nest box and you might convince a bluebird family to move in as neighbors!

DID YOU KNOW?

People put up nest boxes specifically for Western Bluebirds. When people clear land for housing and farming, they often remove dead trees, which means they also remove tree cavities that bluebirds like to nest in. The few tree cavities that remain in an area are sometimes taken over by more aggressive introduced species like House Sparrows and European Starlings. Adding a nest box to a fence line in an area with plenty of tasty insects can provide a Western Bluebird pair a place to live and nest.

MOUNTAIN BLUEBIRD

The state bird of Idaho and the Western Bluebird's all-blue cousin. Found in more mountainous areas, but also in the high desert, this sky-blue bird is often seen perched on fence lines along roads.

TOWNSEND'S SOLITAIRE (BNFB)

Plain gray with a white eye ring. It's in the thrush family (along with bluebirds and robins), but it acts more like a flycatcher. It often perches high in a tree, hunting insects, or it stays hidden in a group of juniper trees, eating berries. It makes a single, clear whistled call and sings a long, jumbly song.

AMRO

American Robin

Turdus migratorius

FIELD MARKS

- Broken white eye ring
- Reddish underparts
- Dark head and back
- Pointy yellow beak

HABITAT
Nearly anywhere—wooded areas, cities, farmland, and marshes

DIET
Invertebrates like insects and worms; fruits and berries

NEST
Sturdy cup of grass, twigs, and mud, lined with grass

CALLS & SONGS
Calls include a *chuk-chuck* and a sharp *yeek*; song is a string of notes that rise and fall, *cheer-up, cheerily, cheer-up, cheerily*

RANGE

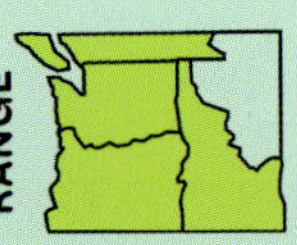

SIZE

Length ~9"
Wingspan ~14"

Most people are familiar with American Robins, because these birds are often seen in yards and parks, pulling worms out of the soil and singing loud, musical songs. In spring, you might find a robin nest in a shrub near your home or school. They often nest close to buildings and raise several clutches (nests of eggs) every year. Look for the pale, spotted juvenile birds when they first leave the nest—you might not recognize them because they don't look like adult robins. Robins sometimes grab live ants and rub them on their feathers and skin, or they lie down in a spot with many ants and let the insects crawl over their bodies. This is called anting—and several bird species do it. Scientists think the ants release chemicals that help keep the birds clean and pest-free. Robins belong to a group of songbirds called thrushes. Several other thrushes live in the Northwest, but they're more secretive than American Robins.

SWAINSON'S THRUSH (BNFB)

Quite shy, plain brown above and spotted below, with a white eye ring. This bird's song is an incredible flute-like melody that spirals up and up.

HERMIT THRUSH

Looks similar to the Swainson's Thrush, but its song is a loud, clear whistle, followed by a jumbled warble of soft, echoing notes. If it isn't singing, you'll need to get a clear look at this bird to identify it based on its reddish tail and paler eye ring.

VEERY

Very secretive and loves to hide in thick vegetation in the woods. Their song is a loud series of trills that spiral downward, almost like the Swainson's Thrush's song played in reverse.

VATH

Varied Thrush

Ixoreus naevius

FIELD MARKS

- Orange eyebrow, throat, and belly
- Dark breast band
- Black and orange wings

HABITAT
Mixed forests

DIET
Insects in summer; nuts and fruits in winter

NEST
Cup of twigs, mud, and rotting wood, lined with soft materials

CALLS & SONGS
Long, buzzy whistles that last a few seconds

RANGE

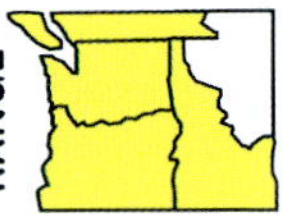

SIZE

S

Length ~9"
Wingspan ~14"

It's exciting to spot the bright orange belly and masked face of a Varied Thrush through a dark and wet Pacific Northwest forest. But it's just as thrilling to hear one belt out its eerie, buzzy whistle when it echoes through the woods. This bird might remind you of an American Robin, but it has an orange eyebrow stripe, an orange throat, and a breast decorated with a dark "necklace." And unlike common robins, Varied Thrushes are more often hidden deep in the woods. In winter, especially when heavy snow covers the hills and mountains, they may visit the valley floor and show up in more neighborhoods.

DID YOU KNOW?

A Varied Thrush nest has an outer layer of sturdy twigs; a middle layer of rotting wood, mud, and grass; and an inner cup made of grass, dead leaves, and fine moss. Pieces of green moss often hang over the edge of a nest, and it's a beautiful thing to find tucked in an evergreen tree in the forest. People often assume that birds live in their nests, since they spend so much time and energy making them. But nests are usually built as a place to incubate eggs and keep chicks safe and warm before they fledge. Outside of nesting season, birds spend evenings roosting in trees, not resting in their nests.

American Pipit

Anthus rubescens

HABITAT
Nests in the tundra; in meadows and other open areas in winter

DIET
Mostly insects

NEST
Cup of grass, lined with soft materials like hair and feathers

CALLS & SONGS
Calls *pi-pit* in flight; song is a series of *twee* notes

RANGE

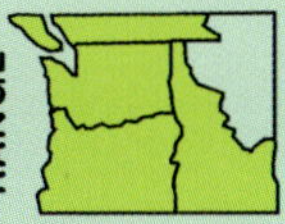

SIZE

Length ~6"
Wingspan ~10"

These small songbirds are often found in farmed fields, meadows, and other open areas. They breed in the Arctic tundra, but in winter in the Pacific Northwest you can sometimes find large flocks walking through open fields, strutting across the ground, searching for food. These rather plain-looking birds blend in well with their surroundings. But when flocks are on the move and flying along, they call almost constantly. If you're able to get a close look at an American Pipit, you may notice that it has a superlong hind toe—probably to help it keep its balance when it walks through mud and snow in the tundra.

FIELD MARKS
- Long tail with white outer feathers
- Streaky breast
- White eye ring
- Pale throat

DID YOU KNOW?
Sometimes birders talk about the GISS (jizz) of a bird, which stands for the "general impressions of size and shape." The American Pipit is a good example of a bird that doesn't have many special field marks or things to look for. It's rather plain and is often viewable only from far away. So how can a birder tell it's a pipit and not some other species like a sparrow or a lark? They often rely on the GISS of this bird—its long tail and short, thin bill, and the way it walks (almost like a little chicken)—to figure out what they're seeing.

Evening Grosbeak

Coccothraustes vespertinus

FIELD MARKS
- Yellow forehead and eyebrow
- White wing patch
- Thick bill
- Black tail and wing feathers

HABITAT
Evergreen forests

DIET
Seeds, fruit, and insects

NEST
Cup of twigs and roots, lined with grasses, lichen, and pine needles

CALLS & SONGS
Loud, piercing *peer* and buzzy chirp; no song

RANGE

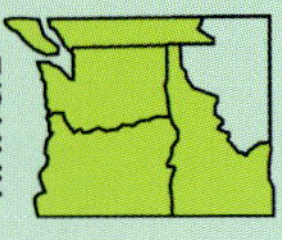

SIZE

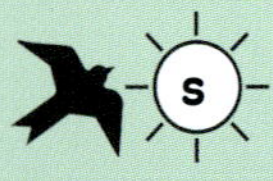

Length ~8"
Wingspan ~13"

A large, noisy flock of these chunky, colorful finches is a welcome sight at any backyard feeder. The male Evening Grosbeak has a brown-and-yellow body, a white inner wing patch, and a bright yellow forehead and eyebrow. Females are mostly gray, with a golden patch on the back of the neck and dark wings and tail. Evening Grosbeaks have massive, seed-crushing bills and can eat an impressive amount of seeds. They're unpredictable and may show up wherever they can find food. Depending on where you live in the Northwest, you might not see any Evening Grosbeaks for years, but then suddenly you can't fill your feeders fast enough!

DID YOU KNOW?

Evening Grosbeaks are songbirds, but they don't really have a song. They make a variety of simple calls, including a loud, sharp chirp and a short, buzzy trill. Even though they don't have a long or complicated song, they often all call at once while traveling in large flocks. When a dozen Evening Grosbeaks fly overhead calling one after another, it can sound quite musical!

GCRF

Gray-crowned Rosy-Finch

Leucosticte tephrocotis

FIELD MARKS

- Gray-and-black face
- Brownish breast
- Pinkish flanks and wings

HABITAT
Mountains

DIET
Seeds and insects

NEST
Cup of moss, lichen, and grass, lined with soft materials like hair and feathers

CALLS & SONGS
Buzzy *choop*, chirps, and squawks

RANGE

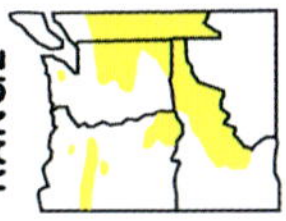

SIZE

Length ~6"
Wingspan ~13"

You might have to hike to the top of a mountain to see this bird, but it's worth the trek! This beautiful finch has a black forehead and a delicate mix of brown and pink feathers on its belly and wings. They prefer high, rocky areas, above the timberline. Visit a mountaintop and you might stumble upon a small flock feeding on the ground. Probably because they rarely see people and aren't afraid, they sometimes feed right on the trail and seem fearless, even as hikers approach. They blend in so well with the ground, you may not notice them until they flush. When flushed, they often circle above before landing in the same spot.

PINE GROSBEAK

A large, colorful finch with a stubby, curved bill that lives in mountain forests. Their plumage color can be bright red, orange, or yellow.

HOFI

House Finch

Haemorhous mexicanus

FIELD MARKS

- Reddish head and breast
- Streaky belly
- Thick bill

HABITAT
Backyards, parks, forests, farms, open grasslands, and deserts

DIET
Seeds, buds, and fruit

NEST
Cup of plant material and feathers, lined with softer materials

CALLS & SONGS
Calls include a *chewp*; song is long and jumbly, ends with a long note that slurs up or down

RANGE

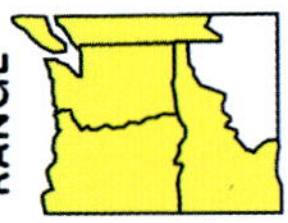

SIZE

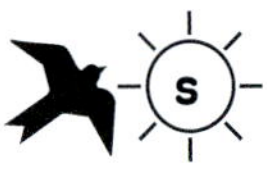

Length ~6"
Wingspan ~9"

This bird is familiar to many people. The House Finch visits backyard feeders and shows up in a wide variety of habitats around the Pacific Northwest. The males have red feathers on their foreheads, throats, bellies, and rumps, though sometimes they can be more orange or even yellow. The females are plain brown and streaky. The House Finch lives close to people, in cities and towns or around farmhouses. They sing a long, jumbly song that ends with a slurred note that either goes up or drops down at the end. Other reddish and streaky finches live in our area, including the Purple Finch and the Cassin's Finch, but they can be tough to identify without a careful look. To identify a finch, pay close attention to the amount and placement of red markings, the shape of the head, and the shape of the beak.

FEMALE HOUSE FINCH

DID YOU KNOW?

The red pigments in a male House Finch's feathers are affected by the food it eats. A bird that eats more red seeds, buds, and fruit will be brighter red, and a bird that eats less red-colored food will be more orange or even yellow.

PURPLE FINCH

A male House Finch might look like it was painted red with a paint-brush, but a male Purple Finch looks like it was dipped in the paint can. These birds are not purple, but they do look a lot like a bulkier, more colorful House Finch. Female Purple Finches are streakier than female House Finches.

CASSIN'S FINCH

(BNFB)

Looks like a House Finch but with a more peaked crown instead of a rounded head. The Cassin's is also less streaky and its song is faster paced.

RECR

Red Crossbill

Loxia curvirostra

FIELD MARKS

- Crisscrossed bill
- Short, notched tail
- Male: reddish body, dark wings
- Female: yellowish, brownish

HABITAT
Conifer forests

DIET
Conifer seeds

NEST
Cup of conifer twigs lined with softer plant materials, feathers, or hair

CALLS & SONGS
Calls include a dry *jip-jip*; song is a series of high-pitched whistles and warbles

RANGE

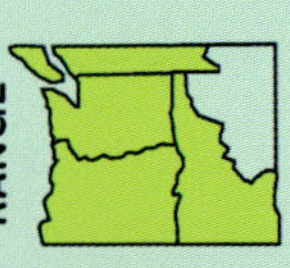

SIZE S

Length ~7"
Wingspan ~10"

This stocky red finch has a short, notched tail and a special bill that crisscrosses when it's closed. It uses its bill to eat the seeds inside conifer cones. It sticks its open bill into the cone and bites down, which opens a space between the cone scales so it can grab the seed inside with its tongue. These birds rely so much on conifer seeds that they don't migrate like other birds. They are nomadic and simply move to whatever area offers the most cones. When they find a place with many cones, even if it's the middle of winter, they might stay there to breed and raise young.

DID YOU KNOW?

The Red Crossbill is changing some of what we know about what makes a species or a subspecies. There are different populations of Red Crossbills with different calls and food preferences. These crossbill "types" all look similar, but they don't seem to mix or breed with one another. Maybe each type is a subspecies, or maybe each is a separate species. Or maybe we are watching subspecies evolving to become separate species!

PISI

Pine Siskin

Spinus pinus

FIELD MARKS

- Sharp, pointy bill
- Yellow on wings
- Streaky all over

HABITAT
Mixed forests

DIET
Seeds of conifers, deciduous trees, grasses, and more

NEST
Bowl of twigs and other plant material, lined with softer items

CALLS & SONGS
Calls include a harsh, rising *zeet* that can sound like a zipper; song is a wheezy string of trills and short notes

RANGE

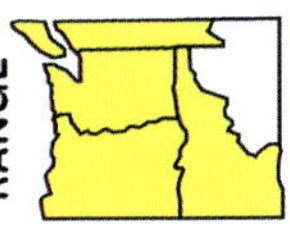

SIZE

Length ~5"
Wingspan ~8"

These streaky little finches are brownish gray with splashes of yellow in the wings and tail. In some winters, Pine Siskins will show up at backyard feeders in large groups and squabble over food. They're nomadic (they wander around in search of food) and erratic (you can't predict when and where they will go next). You'll often hear them before you see them, as they make their rising wheezy calls that sound a bit like a zipper being zipped.

DID YOU KNOW?
Some species, like Pine Siskins, are nomadic and move to wherever they find food. These species don't migrate the way other birds do, and they're described as being "irruptive." This means that in some years, Pine Siskins stay in one habitat or area, and in other years, they irrupt into different areas. One year, you may not see many of these birds, but in other years, your bird feeders might be covered with noisy, bickering siskins!

AGOL

American Goldfinch

Spinus tristis

FIELD MARKS
- Black wings with white wing bars
- Short, pointed bill
- Notched tail

HABITAT
Fields and open areas; suburbs and backyards

DIET
Almost entirely seeds

NEST
Small cup of tightly woven plant material

CALLS & SONGS
Po-ta-to-chip! calls; song is a series of twitters and *swee* notes

RANGE

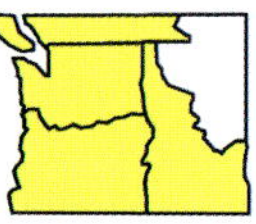

SIZE XS

Length ~5"
Wingspan ~8"

Washington's state bird, the American Goldfinch, is a bright yellow songbird with a notched tail, a pointed bill, and white wing bars. The males look different from females, and both have plumage that changes with the seasons. During breeding season, males are neon-yellow with a black forehead and black wings, and in winter they're paler yellow, sometimes almost white, with black wings. The American Goldfinch's song is a series of cheery trills and *swee* notes, and its flight call sounds a bit like *po-ta-to-chip!*

LESSER GOLDFINCH

(WINTER)

Looks a lot like the American Goldfinch, but the Lesser is smaller than the American and not as bright yellow. In summer, the male Lesser Goldfinch has a dark cap. Its banding code, LEGO, is sometimes used as a nickname for the bird because it's fun to say.

SNBU

Snow Bunting

Plectrophenax nivalis

FIELD MARKS
- Stubby bill
- White and rust-colored plumage
- Black wingtips

HABITAT
Open areas like beaches, dunes, and prairies

DIET
Seeds and insects

NEST
Cup of grass and moss lined with plant material, fur, and feathers

CALLS & SONGS
Calls are clear, whistled *choo* and a musical rattle

RANGE

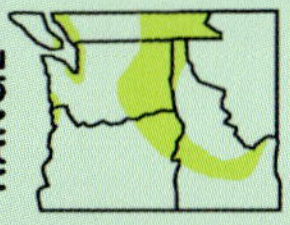

SIZE S

Length ~7"
Wingspan ~14"

When this bird returns to its arctic breeding grounds, the temperatures are below freezing and the ground is covered in snow. Snow Buntings build nests between or under rocks, or they find old barrels, cans, or other rubble to nest in or under. Their crisp black-and-white plumage is fitting for the Far North. When they come to the Pacific Northwest in winter, they're wearing their winter plumage—white feathers with rust-colored patches on their head and breast—and are often described as looking a bit like little toasted marshmallows. Finding a small flock of Snow Buntings at the beach, or a single bird mixed in with Horned Larks inland, is a rare and special treat.

LAPLAND LONGSPUR

Another small songbird that breeds on the Arctic tundra. In breeding plumage, the male has a black face, a thick white eyebrow, and a red nape. At other times of year, these birds look like streaky sparrows. You might spot one or more in an open field or at the beach, often in flocks with Horned Larks or Snow Buntings.

DEJU

Dark-eyed Junco

Junco hyemalis

HABITAT
Breeds in forests; winters in variety of habitats

DIET
Mostly seeds

NEST
Hidden on the ground, made of twigs and lined with fine material

CALLS & SONGS
High, quick chip notes; song is a long trill

RANGE

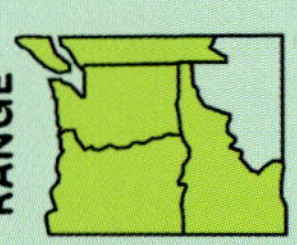

SIZE S

Length ~6"
Wingspan ~9"

These little sparrows are sometimes called "snowbirds," especially in winter when they come down from the mountains to more populated areas, where they often hang around backyard feeders. There are several subspecies of Dark-eyed Juncos (JUN-koze), and they look different enough from one another that some were once thought to be completely separate species. In the Northwest, we see Slate-colored, Gray-headed, Pink-sided, and Oregon juncos, each with different plumage. The Oregon Junco has a black hood, brown body, and white belly. All juncos have pale bills and white outer tail feathers that they flash open when they fly and while they're feeding on the ground.

FIELD MARKS
- Pinkish bill
- Dark hood
- White outer tail feathers

DID YOU KNOW?
Dark-eyed Juncos are one of several birds that regularly flash their tail feathers. Why do they do this? Scientists think birds might flash their tails to show predators that they're alert and ready to move quickly, or maybe they do this to warn other birds of potential danger. Some birds may flick their tails open as a way of flushing small prey up off the ground or off a branch.

SPTO

Spotted Towhee

Pipilo maculatus

FIELD MARKS
- Red eyes
- Dark head
- White belly
- Reddish flanks

HABITAT
Places with dense shrubs to hide in and leaf litter to scratch in

DIET
Insects and seeds

NEST
Stems and leaves, with an inner cup of grasses and hair, on the ground or in a tree

CALLS & SONGS
Catlike *mew* calls; trilling *drink-your-tea!* song

RANGE

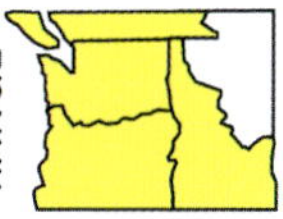

SIZE S

Length ~8"
Wingspan ~11"

This sparrow is large and unique looking, with a thick bill, long tail, and bright red eyes. If a Spotted Towhee (TOE-hee) is hidden away in thick brush, you can hear it loudly scratching through the leaf litter. It hops forward and then backward with both feet, kicking a layer of litter aside to look for insects and seeds. They're also often seen in backyards and under bird feeders. Learn to recognize the sounds of this common bird foraging on the ground and its catlike *mew* call, and you're likely to see Spotted Towhees in many places. In spring, the males are much easier to spot, as they perch high up in shrubs, singing *drink-your-tea!*

GREEN-TAILED TOWHEE

Lives in drier areas in Idaho and eastern Oregon. It has a white throat, a greenish back and tail, and a bright reddish crown.

SOSP

Song Sparrow

Melospiza melodia

FIELD MARKS

- Long, rounded tail
- Gray eyebrow
- Brown stripe through eye
- Streaky breast and belly

HABITAT	DIET	NEST	CALLS & SONGS
Almost anywhere	Insects and seeds	Cup of plant material, lined with grass and animal hair	Call is a loud *cheep!*; song is a few single notes, a buzzy sound, and then a long trill

RANGE

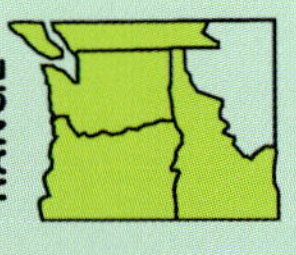

SIZE S

Length ~6"
Wingspan ~8"

This streaky brown sparrow is one of the first bird species you should learn to identify, because they seem to be almost everywhere. There are several subspecies, and they can have unique plumage, but all have streaky brown feathers, with a short bill, a round head, and a long tail. Most have a grayish eyebrow, a darker mustache, and a white throat. If you see a streaky brown bird flitting through the brush or flying low across an open area pumping its tail, it's probably a Song Sparrow. The song starts with a few clear, single notes, then a buzzy sound, and then a long trill. The call is a loud *cheep!*

DID YOU KNOW?

Sparrows are another group of similar-looking birds, so identification can be overwhelming for a new birder. Spend time studying and observing the most common species in your area and get to know them well. These species are, after all, the birds you're going to see most often! Once you can identify a Song Sparrow or Chipping Sparrow quickly and easily at a distance, you're far more likely to notice a sparrow that looks a bit different. Also, if you take the time to learn the songs and calls of the most common birds, a new and unfamiliar song will stop you in your tracks. You may not know what you're hearing at that moment, but you'll have a new bird to investigate.

CHIPPING SPARROW

Has a bright reddish crown, a black line through the eye, and a plain gray belly.

Other Sparrows

Sparrows are part of a group of birds that some birders call LBBs—little brown birds. At first, all sparrows may seem little and brown, but if you look closely at their detailed plumage and the various stripes and markings on their faces, and you begin to learn their beautiful songs, you can slowly get to know all the LBBs that live in your area. Start by learning to identify the most common sparrows in your patch. Then you can compare any new birds you see to those you already know. Also, if you focus on a single field mark to look for on each species, any special or unusual mark might help you identify each bird. Many kinds of sparrows live in the Pacific Northwest. Most of them have different plumage at different times of year and at different times in their lives. A sparrow in summer plumage may not look the same in winter, and juvenile sparrows can be tough to identify for a new birder.

FOX SPARROW

Big and dark, with thick, triangle-shaped brown marks on its breast

AMERICAN TREE SPARROW

Reddish crown and a reddish stripe through each eye, a gray face, and a bill that's brown on top and yellow on the bottom

GOLDEN-CROWNED SPARROW

Golden crown and thick black eyebrows

WHITE-CROWNED SPARROW

Black-and-white–striped crown and a black line through each eye

SAVANNAH SPARROW

Small and pale, with fine brown streaking on its breast and a yellow stripe above each eye

LINCOLN'S SPARROW (BNFB)

Tiny bird with grayish face, pale ring around each eye, and fine streaks on its breast

WHITE-THROATED SPARROW

Resembles a White-crowned Sparrow but has a white throat and a yellow spot between the bill and each eye

SAGEBRUSH SPARROW

Gray face, white eye rings, a white spot in front of each eye, and a habit of running on the ground with its tail held up

BREWER'S SPARROW (BNFB)

Pale plumage with a brown crown and white eye rings

LARK SPARROW

Face is striped in white, reddish, and black; has a dark spot on its gray breast

GRASSHOPPER SPARROW

Small and compact, with a flat head, yellow markings, and dark crown stripes

VESPER SPARROW

Bold white eye rings and a pale mustache

Bobolink

Dolichonyx oryzivorus

FIELD MARKS
- Dark overall
- Cream-colored nape
- White rump
- White wing patches

HABITAT
Open, damp meadows

DIET
Seeds, insects, and small invertebrates

NEST
Woven grass and other plant material, on the ground

CALLS & SONGS
Call is a metallic *tink*; male's song is rambling and bubbly with squeaky high notes and low buzzes

RANGE

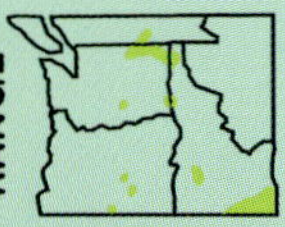

SIZE

Length ~7"
Wingspan ~12"

In summer, Bobolinks (BOB-uh-links) breed in a few spots in the Pacific Northwest, and visiting one of these spots to see this unusual bird is well worth your time. The male looks like a blackbird with big white patches on its wings and rump and a cream-colored patch on the back of its head (or nape). The female looks like an oversized sparrow, with dark crown stripes and pale eyebrows. If you're lucky, you might catch the male doing its entertaining courtship display. He perches on a plant or post, and then flies around the area fluttering his wings and singing a rambling, bubbly song full of high squeaks and low buzzes.

MALE BOBOLINK

FEMALE BOBOLINK

DID YOU KNOW?

Bobolinks make one of the most impressive migrations of any songbird, traveling more than 12,000 miles back and forth to southern South America each year. Not only is their migration remarkably long for a small songbird, but they may use the stars to find their way! Experiments done in a planetarium show that the Bobolink uses the stars to decide which direction to travel. Scientists also found that small amounts of magnetic materials in their heads may help them use Earth's magnetic field to navigate on their long journeys!

WEME

Western Meadowlark

Sturnella neglecta

HABITAT
Open grasslands and fields

DIET
Seeds and insects

NEST
Cup dug into the ground, lined with dry grass; sometimes topped by a woven grass dome

CALLS & SONGS
Call is a low *jup*; songs are clear whistles and quick warbling notes that drop in pitch

RANGE

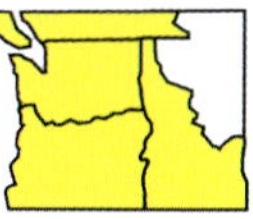

SIZE S

Length ~8"
Wingspan ~16"

Oregon's state bird, the Western Meadowlark, is a short-tailed grassland bird with bright yellow underparts. For many birders, its song is the soundtrack of the prairie. A Western Meadowlark's flute-like song is made up of clear whistles and quick warbling notes that drop in pitch. Often heard singing from deep in a grassy area, the Western Meadowlark is a bird worth looking for. It has a distinct black V-shaped necklace on its bright yellow breast, dark stripes on its crown, pale eyebrows, and a long, pointy bill. There's something about the Western Meadowlark that people like—it's the state bird of six states!

FIELD MARKS
- Flat head
- Long, pointy bill
- Yellow underparts
- Black bib and spotting

DID YOU KNOW?
Despite being mottled brown on top and bright yellow underneath, meadowlarks are members of the blackbird (Icteridae) family. Like its blackbird cousins, a meadowlark often feeds by gaping—sticking its bill into the soil and opening it to create a small hole. This helps the bird reach small insects and seeds hidden underneath. Birds that feed in this way will also stick their bills into fruits or into larger insects and then open their bills to eat what's inside.

BUOR

Bullock's Oriole (BNFB)

Icterus bullockii

HABITAT
Open woodlands, especially along rivers

DIET
Insects, fruit, and nectar

NEST
Hanging woven pouch made of plants, grass, hair, and twine

CALLS & SONGS
Call a harsh chatter; song is full of whistles, rattles, and scratchy, squeaky notes

RANGE

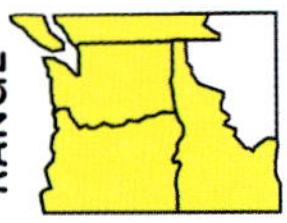

SIZE

Length ~8"
Wingspan ~12"

This bright orange bird is known for its loud, chattering calls and its remarkable hanging nest. Look and listen for the Bullock's Oriole in spring and summer, in open areas with clumps of trees, especially along rivers. You may see one high in a tree, snatching insects from branches, or hanging upside down while it looks for food. They also love to eat fruit and drink nectar. Male and female Bullock's Orioles both sing, but their songs aren't quite the same. Females tend to sing more frequently, but the males' song sounds sweeter.

FIELD MARKS
- Black cap and eye lines
- Long, pointy beak
- White wing patch

DID YOU KNOW?

Bullock's Orioles don't visit typical bird feeders full of seeds or suet, but they will sometimes drink from a hummingbird feeder. They often drink nectar from flowers, so it makes sense that they would visit a hummingbird feeder full of sugar water. You can also attract Bullock's Orioles to your yard by putting out orange halves or a container of watered-down grape jelly. In fact, many birding stores sell special oriole feeders that have a place built in for fruit, mealworms, and jellies.

Red-winged Blackbird

Agelaius phoeniceus

FIELD MARKS
- Red and yellow shoulder patches
- Thick, pointy bill
- Glossy black plumage

HABITAT
Marshes and wetlands, neighborhoods, and farmlands

DIET
Seeds and insects

NEST
Cup of mud and plant material, lined with grass, near the ground in dense vegetation

CALLS & SONGS
Metallic whistled and buzzy calls; *konk-a-ree* song

RANGE

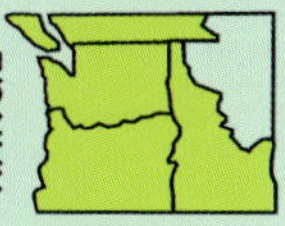

SIZE S

Length ~8"
Wingspan ~14"

The male Red-winged Blackbird is perfectly named—it's a black bird with red wing patches! Those patches with yellow borders underneath are called *epaulets*, named after the ornamental shoulder pieces on military uniforms. In spring, males puff up and sing, showing off their epaulets to attract mates and intimidate rivals. Females are tough to identify, since they aren't black and don't have any red on their wings! They look like large, streaky sparrows and often confuse new birders.

YELLOW-HEADED BLACKBIRD

Larger than a Red-winged Blackbird, with a yellow head and breast.

BREWER'S BLACKBIRD (BNFB)

So glossy it can look purplish or black, depending on the lighting. It has no wing patch, and the male has bright yellow eyes.

BHCO

Brown-headed Cowbird

Molothrus ater

FIELD MARKS
- Brown head
- Shiny black body
- Sharp beak

HABITAT
Open areas, towns, and city parks

DIET
Insects and seeds

NEST
Other birds' nests

CALLS & SONGS
Females make a chatter call; males sing liquid-sounding notes and whistles

Length ~8"
Wingspan ~12"

These brown-headed birds used to follow bison herds as they moved across the plains, eating the insects that the big animals stirred up. Because of that nomadic lifestyle, Brown-headed Cowbirds evolved to be brood parasites—animals that rely on other animals to raise their young. So instead of building a nest and incubating her own eggs, the female lays eggs in another bird's nest and the chicks are "adopted" and raised by the other bird! They often deposit their eggs in the nests of smaller songbirds like Yellow Warblers and Warbling Vireos.

DID YOU KNOW?

After a Brown-headed Cowbird lays her eggs in another bird's nest, the nest owner may recognize the eggs as different from its own and either push the eggs out or start a whole new nest. But many birds don't seem to notice at all. Brown-headed Cowbird eggs often hatch faster than the host bird's eggs, so the cowbird chicks end up being older and bigger than their nestmates. This can mean that the cowbird chicks get most of the food brought by parents, which isn't good news for the other nestlings. This spring, keep your eyes peeled for a small songbird struggling to feed its much larger cowbird kid!

BHGR

Black-headed Grosbeak

Pheucticus melanocephalus

FIELD MARKS
- Black head
- Orange collar, belly, and rump
- White wing spots

HABITAT
Mixed forests and city parks

DIET
Seeds, fruits, and insects

NEST
Loose clump of twigs and stems with an inner cup of plant material

CALLS & SONGS
Sweeter, slurred version of a robin's song

RANGE

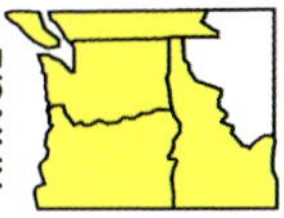

SIZE

S

Length ~8"
Wingspan ~12"

Learn to recognize the songs and calls of these songbirds, and you're bound to hear them in spring and summer. Listen for a song that rises and falls like a robin's song but is quicker, with sweeter, more slurred notes. Their sharp *peek* calls sound like squeaky door hinges. If you hear its call, look for a bird with a beautiful mix of orange, black, and white feathers and a thick, triangle-shaped bill. It may be foraging high in the trees. Males are bright orange with a black head, and females are brownish with a dark head and pale eyebrows.

DID YOU KNOW?

People often wonder why male birds tend to be colorful and female birds tend to be plain looking—sometimes they can even look like two separate species! In most cases, the male is putting his time and energy into looking and sounding healthy to attract a female mate. The female often needs to blend in with her nest and its surroundings while she incubates eggs and tends chicks. Though male Black-headed Grosbeaks are more colorful than females, both parents split parenting duties equally, taking turns incubating eggs, feeding chicks, and defending the nest.

COYE

Common Yellowthroat

Geothlypis trichas

FIELD MARKS

- Large round head
- Black mask under white stripe
- Yellow belly
- Long tail

HABITAT
Wet areas with thick vegetation

DIET
Insects and spiders

NEST
Cup of grass, sometimes with a woven roof

CALLS & SONGS
Thick, low *chuck* call; distinct *witchity-witchity-witchity* song

RANGE

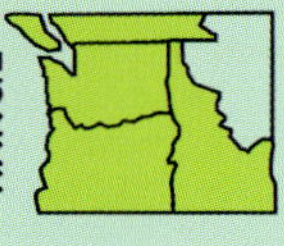

SIZE XS

Length ~5"
Wingspan ~6"

Learn to recognize the *witchity-witchity-witchity* song of this little masked warbler and it will be one of the most common songs you hear in wetlands each spring and summer. Even though this bird likes to hide in thick vegetation, the male really stands out with his bright yellow belly and throat and wide black mask. Females don't have a mask, are a paler yellow, and can sometimes look similar to an Orange-crowned Warbler. If you hear this bird's song on your next walk, stop and look around for a moment. You might see a Common Yellowthroat pop up to sing or spot one flying low along the ground between plant thickets.

YELLOW-BREASTED CHAT

Another species you may hear singing loudly on a spring bird walk—but may find hard to see clearly. Like the Common Yellowthroat, it has a bright yellow belly and throat. Try to get a clear view of this bird through your binoculars. It's quite large—almost 8 inches long—and sort of like a giant warbler. Its song is very distinct—a strange mix of croaking noises, rattles, and whistles, and it mimics other birds' sounds too. They're famous for singing for hours on end, sometimes even in the middle of the night!

YRWA

Yellow-rumped Warbler

Setophaga coronata

FIELD MARKS

- Yellow crown patch and rump
- Yellow side patch
- White or yellow throat

HABITAT
Wide variety of habitats

DIET
Insects and berries

NEST
Cup of twigs, grass, and pine needles lined with hair and feathers

CALLS & SONGS
Slow warble that rises at the end (Audubon's subspecies), or musical trill (Myrtle subspecies)

RANGE

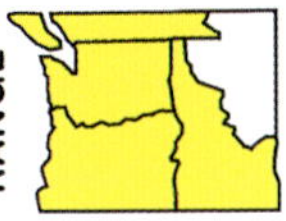

SIZE

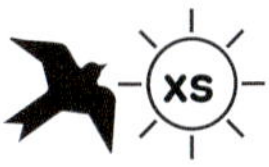

Length ~5"
Wingspan ~9"

Because of its rump patch, which is the color and shape of a pad of butter, this bird is sometimes called a "butterbutt." It also has a yellow crown patch and yellow patches on its sides. You can find these large warblers with short bills and long tails in a tree, sometimes in a loose flock, either picking off insects directly from leaves and branches or flying out to catch bugs on the wing before landing again. Yellow-rumped Warblers will also visit bird feeders, especially if you put out suet cakes (blocks of seeds held together by fat). Once you know their dry *check* calls, you'll hear them all the time, especially during migration!

AUDUBON'S SUBSPECIES

MYRTLE SUBSPECIES

Today, there are two subspecies of Yellow-rumped Warbler, but scientists used to think they were two separate species. The Myrtle subspecies is more common in the eastern United States, and Audubon's is more common in the west, though you can see both in the Pacific Northwest. Myrtle has a white throat and Audubon's has a yellow throat.

YEWA

Yellow Warbler

Setophaga petechia

FIELD MARKS

- Heavy bill
- Lemon-yellow head
- Black eyes
- Reddish belly streaking

HABITAT
Wetlands and woods along streams

DIET
Mostly insects

NEST
Cup of plant material lined with soft fibers like deer hair, feathers, and dandelion seeds

CALLS & SONGS
Calls include buzzy chip notes; song sounds like *sweet, sweet, aren't I so sweet?*

RANGE

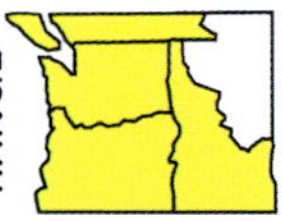

SIZE

Length ~5"
Wingspan ~8"

Warblers are known for being small and brightly colored but difficult to see. That's because they tend to move quickly through the treetops and are often hidden behind leaves. The Yellow Warbler is no different. Even though it's a bright lemon-yellow, it can be tough to spot! Luckily, it sings often during spring and summer and its song is easy to remember: a series of notes that sounds like *sweet, sweet, sweet, aren't I so sweet?* When you hear that song, it's worth investigating. Getting a clear view of a Yellow Warbler, especially when it drops down to near eye level, is worth the extra effort. Plus, you don't want to spend too much time looking up at the treetops. When birders do that for too long, they end up with a special type of sore neck called warbler neck!

DID YOU KNOW?

Brown-headed Cowbirds often lay their eggs in Yellow Warbler nests, and the warblers often raise the cowbird chicks. But sometimes Yellow Warblers recognize these eggs as different from their own, and instead of pushing the cowbird eggs out, they build a whole new nest on top of the old one. Sometimes a cowbird will return and lay eggs in the warbler's new nest, and the warbler will build yet another nest. Yellow Warblers have been known to build up to six nests stacked one on top of the other!

(BNFB) WILSON'S WARBLER

Looks like a Yellow Warbler wearing a black cap. Instead of foraging high in the trees, this bird often feeds low to the ground. Even though it moves fast, it can be easier to spot than some of the other warblers. Its song is a series of loud *tsee* notes that drop in pitch.

Other Warblers

Warblers are often among birders' favorite birds. They're energetic and colorful, and they can be difficult to find. Most don't visit feeders, but they are found in a wide variety of habitats. Learning warbler songs is important because these birds are often easier to hear than see. It's a challenge to get a close look at a warbler or get a clear photograph of one.

ORANGE-CROWNED WARBLER

Common warbler in the Northwest is usually greenish yellow overall (some are more yellow and some more gray), with pale eyebrows and small orange crown that's often hard to see

MACGILLIVRAY'S WARBLER (BNFB)

Likes to skulk in thick vegetation and can be tough to find, with a gray head and breast, a yellow body, and white arcs above and below each eye

BLACK-THROATED GRAY WARBLER

Boldly patterned in black and white, with a bright yellow spot between its eyes and bill

HERMIT WARBLER

Often heard and not seen, with a bright yellow face and black throat; a special bird not found in many other places

NASHVILLE WARBLER

Beautiful warbler with a gray head, a yellow belly, and a bright white ring around each eye

TOWNSEND'S WARBLER (BNFB)

A welcome sight on a dreary winter day, with a high-contrast pattern of bright yellow and black markings; will visit backyard feeders

WETA

Western Tanager

Piranga ludoviciana

HABITAT
Almost anywhere; nests in mountain forests

DIET
Insects and berries

NEST
Loose bowl of twigs, with a small cup inside made of grass, hair, and feathers

CALLS & SONGS
Song like a robin's (*cheer-up, cheer-up, cheer-up*) but choppier and hoarser

RANGE

SIZE

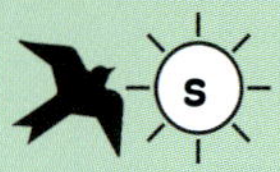

Length ~7"
Wingspan ~11"

One of the most colorful songbirds to visit the Pacific Northwest, the male Western Tanager has a bright yellow body and a reddish head. Its wings, back, and tail are black. Even though they prefer forests and mountains, Western Tanagers can show up in backyards and parks, even in cities. New birders are often surprised to learn that these tropical-looking birds live in our area. Though it's brightly colored, the Western Tanager can be tough to spot because it usually feeds on insects high in trees. Learn to recognize its song, which is like a robin's song but choppy, sharp, and hoarse. If you hear it, start scanning the trees, because this bird is beautiful!

FIELD MARKS
- Reddish head
- Yellow underparts
- Pale wing bars
- Black wings and tail

DID YOU KNOW?
Most birds with red feathers get those pigments from the plants that they eat. But Western Tanagers seem to do things differently. Scientists believe these birds get their beautiful red head feathers from a rare pigment in the insects they eat!

LAZB

Lazuli Bunting

Passerina amoena

FIELD MARKS

- Bright blue head
- White wing bars
- Pumpkin-colored chest patch
- White belly

HABITAT
Brushy, open areas, often near a river or creek

DIET
Insects and seeds

NEST
Cup of grass, bark, and leaves, close to the ground in a tree or shrub

CALLS & SONGS
Series of jumbled, squeaky, repeated notes

RANGE

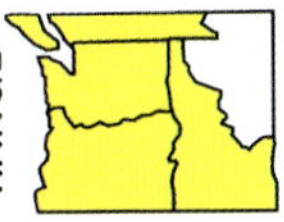

SIZE XS

Length ~5"
Wingspan ~9"

Nothing says summer birding in the Pacific Northwest like a bright turquoise Lazuli Bunting perched out in the open, singing its jumbling song. Named after lapis lazuli, a rock known for its unique blue color, the male Lazuli Bunting has an electric-blue head and back, a pumpkin-colored chest patch, and a white belly. Females are a muted gray-brown with just a bit of orange on the chest and a touch of blue in the wings and tail. This songbird is shaped like a small finch, with a cone-shaped bill and a notched tail. Look for them in brushy areas, especially near a river or creek, and enjoy their song on a sunny summer day.

DID YOU KNOW?

Every male Lazuli Bunting sings a unique song. When young males first migrate to the areas where they breed, they listen to the older males singing nearby. Then they borrow parts of the different songs they hear, rearrange some of the notes, and sing their own version! Lazuli Buntings that live in one area will all sing similar songs because they copy one another and learn from neighbors, just as people from certain places have an accent or a particular way of speaking.

ACKNOWLEDGMENTS

Thank you to all the photographers who generously contributed their work to this project, including Audrey Addison, Andrew Aldrich, Andrew Boycott, Angela Calabrese, Alan Schmierer, Ali VanderGrift, Blair Dudeck, Brad Imhoff, Becky Matsubara, Brian Sullivan, Brad Vissia, Carl Bergstrom, Chuck Gates, Colton Veltkamp, Chris S. Wood, Darren Clark, Daniel Irons, Drew Beamer, Elliott Bury, Ethan Denton, Eric Ellingson, Erica Heusser, Evan Larson, Evan Lipton, Frank Lin, Gerry Meenaghan, Jackie Bowman, Judy Gallagher, Joshua Little, Jim Moodie, John Reynolds, Jen Sanford, Janine Schutt, Ken Chamberlain, Kyle Landstra, Kalin Ocaña, Ken Pitts, Katie Warner, Liam Huber, Liam Hutcheson, Luke Seitz, Matthew Dolkart, Melissa Hafting, Mason Maron, Marky Mutchler, Nik Teichmann, Nigel Tate, Philip Kline, Russ Morgan, Rain Saulnier, Sasha Cahill, Scott Carpenter, Scott Heron, Steven McGrath, Stephanie Stragier, Tara Lemezis, Tanner Martin, and Vasura Jayaweera.

Thanks to Drew for running our bakery, to my family for listening to me talk about birds for the last eight years, to Kayla for advice, to K Wray for edits, and to all my students, past and present, for inspiring me to keep learning. And thanks to the folks at Timber: Will for getting this project started, Ryan for moving it along, Cobi for problem solving, and Lisa for making it better.

BIBLIOGRAPHY

Bent, A. C. 1938. *Life Histories of North American Birds of Prey*. Part 2, *Orders Falconiformes and Strigiformes*. *Bulletin of the United States National Museum* i–viii, 1–492.

Billerman, S. M., B. K. Keeney, P. G. Rodewald, and T. S. Schulenberg, eds. 2022. *Birds of the World*. Ithaca, NY: Cornell Laboratory of Ornithology. birdsoftheworld.org/bow/home.

Dunn, J. L., and J. K. Alderfer. 2017. *National Geographic Field Guide to the Birds of North America*, 7th ed. Washington, DC: National Geographic.

Shewey, J., and T. Blount. 2017. *Birds of the Pacific Northwest*. Portland, OR: Timber Press.

Sibley, D. 2003. *The Sibley Field Guide to Birds of Western North America*, 1st ed. New York: Alfred A. Knopf.

American Bittern:

Chapin, J. P. 1922. The function of the oesophagus in the bittern's booming. *The Auk* 39:196–202.

American Wigeon:

Wishart, R. A. 1985. Moult chronology of American Wigeon, *Anas americana*, in relation to reproduction. *Canadian Field-Naturalist* 99:172–178.

Anna's Hummingbird:

Clark, C. J., and S. M. Russell. 2020. Anna's Hummingbird (*Calypte anna*), version 1.0. In *Birds of the World* (A. F. Poole, ed). Ithaca, NY: Cornell Laboratory of Ornithology.

Bewick's Wren:

Baumgartner, F. M., and A. M. Baumgartner. 1992. *Oklahoma Bird Life*. Norman, OK: University of Oklahoma Press.

Black-billed Magpie:

Ryser, F. A. Jr. 1985. *Birds of the Great Basin: A Natural History.* Reno, NV: University of Nevada Press.

Bobolink:

Beason, R. C., and J. E. Nichols. 1984. Magnetic orientation and magnetically sensitive material in a transequatorial migratory bird. *Nature* 309:151–153.

California Quail:

Campbell, R. W., N. K. Dawe, I. McTaggart-Cowan, et al. 1990. *The Birds of British Columbia*. Vol. 2, *Nonpasserines: Diurnal Birds of Prey Through Woodpeckers*. Victoria, BC: Royal British Columbia Museum.

Cedar Waxwing:

Hudon, J., and A. H. Brush. 1989. Probable dietary basis of a color variant of the Cedar Waxwing. *Journal of Field Ornithology* 60:361–368.

Common Loon:

Nocera, J. J., and N. M. Burgess. 2002. Diving schedules of Common Loons in varying environments. *Canadian Journal of Zoology* 80(9):1643–1648.

Hooded Merganser:

Sivak, J. G., and R. F. Glover. 1986. Anatomy of the avian membrana nictitans. *Canadian Journal of Zoology* 64:963–972.

Mallard:

Palmer, R. S. 1976. *Handbook of North American Birds*. Vol. 2, *Waterfowl*. New Haven, CT: Yale University Press.

Mourning Dove:

Richkus, K. D., M. T. Moore, P. I. Padding, and E. M. Martin. 2007. Migratory bird hunting activity and harvest during the 2005 and 2006 hunting seasons: Preliminary estimates. Washington, DC: US Fish and Wildlife Service.

Northern Pygmy-Owl:

Steyn, P. 1979. Observations on Pearl-spotted and Barred owls. *Bokmakierie* 31:50–60.

Osprey:

Machmer, M. M., and R. C. Ydenberg. 1990. Weather and Osprey foraging energetics. *Canadian Journal of Zoology* 68:40–43.

Peregrine Falcon:

Orton, D. A. 1975. The speed of a Peregrine's dive. *The Field* 25: 588–590.

Red-breasted Nuthatch:

Tyler, W. M. 1948. Red-breasted Nuthatch. In *Life Histories of North American Nuthatches, Wrens, Thrashers, and Their Allies*. (A. C. Bent, ed.) US National Museum Bulletin 195:22–35.

Tufted Puffin:

Wehle, D. H. S. 1983. The food, feeding and development of young Tufted and Horned puffins in Alaska. *Condor* 85:427–442.

Tundra Swan:

Scott, D. 1978. Social behaviour of wintering Bewick's Swans. PhD thesis, University of Cambridge.

Western Grebe:

Piersma, T., and M. R. Van Eerden. 1989. Feather eating in Great Crested Grebes *Podiceps cristatus*: a unique solution to the problem of debris and gastric parasites in fish-eating birds. *Ibis* 131:477–486.

Western Meadowlark:

Orians, G. H. 1985. *Blackbirds of the Americas*. Seattle: University of Washington Press.

Western Tanager:

Hudon, J. 1990. Unusual carotenoid use by the Western Tanager (*Piranga ludoviciana*) and its evolutionary implications. *Canadian Journal of Zoology* 69:2311–2320.

White-faced Ibis:

Kotter, B. L. 1970. An ecological natural history of the White-faced Ibis (*Plegadis chihi*) in northern Utah. Master's thesis, University of Utah.

Yellow Warbler:

Berger, A. J. 1955. Six-storied Yellow Warbler nest with 11 cowbird eggs. *Jack-Pine Warbler* 33:84.

PHOTOGRAPHY & ILLUSTRATION CREDITS

Photographs are by **Tom Myers** with the exception of the following:

Audrey Addison, page 75 bottom right, page 109, page 118

Andrew Aldrich, page 26 bottom left and bottom right, page 27 bottom left

Andrew Boycott, page 97 bottom

Angela Calabrese, page 63 top right, page 65 bottom

Ali VanderGrift, page 21 bottom, page 61 bottom right, page 78 top

Blair Dudeck, page 24 bottom, page 29 top, page 39 top and center, page 73 top

Brad Imhoff, page 25 bottom, page 26 top right, page 27 top and center right, page 53 bottom

Becky Matsubara, page 19 top, page 30, page 34, page 131 bottom left, page 144, page 153

Brian Sullivan, page 101 bottom right, page 103 bottom

Brad Vissia, page 100 bottom, page 115 bottom left, page 127 bottom

Carl Bergstrom, page 23 bottom, page 27 center left, page 31 bottom

Chuck Gates, page 65 top, page 67 bottom, page 101 bottom left, page 121 top row, page 152 bottom right, page 180 bottom left, page 192

Colton Veltkamp, page 69 bottom

Chris S. Wood, page 19 bottom

Drew Beamer, page 176

Darren Clark, page 74 top right, page 75 top right, center left, center right and bottom left, page 175 bottom

Daniel Irons, page 79, page 137 bottom

Elliott Bury, page 83 bottom, page 152 top right, page 173, page 180 bottom right

Ethan Denton, page 74 top left, bottom left and bottom right, page 75 top left

Eric Ellingson, page 29 bottom, page 71, page 72, page 73 bottom

Erica Heusser, page 63 center left, page 165 bottom, page 199 top
Evan Larson, page 33 top, page 37 top right, page 180 top
Evan Lipton, page 26 top left
Frank Lin, page 29 center right, page 31 top, page 33 bottom, page 49 bottom
Gerry Meenaghan, page 37 bottom left, page 107, page 186 top right
Jackie Bowman, page 76
Joshua Little, page 142
Jim Moodie, page 45 top, page 100 top right, page 121 bottom, page 171 center
John Reynolds, page 27 bottom right, page 83 center, page 152 bottom left
Jen Sanford, page 45 center, page 143 top
Janine Schutt, page 138 top, page 145, page 198 top right
Ken Chamberlain, page 36 bottom, page 42 bottom, page 113, page 131 bottom right
Kyle Landstra, page 81 bottom right, page 133 top right
Kalin Ocaña, page 77 bottom, page 124 bottom right, page 159 bottom
Ken Pitts, page 96, page 127 top, page 103 top
Katie Warner, page 141 top
Liam Huber, page 77 top, page 101 top left
Liam Hutcheson, page 37 bottom right, page 88 bottom
Luke Seitz, page 132 left
Matthew Dolkart, page 41 center right
Melissa Hafting, page 22, page 32, page 157 bottom
Mason Maron, page 41 top left, page 117, page 128 bottom, page 136
Marky Mutchler, page 49 center, page 51 center, page 78 bottom, page 128 top
Nik Teichmann, page 33 center
Philip Kline, page 186 bottom left
Russ Morgan, page 38, page 62 top left, page 164, page 175 top, page 181 bottom
Rain Saulnier, page 138 bottom
Sasha Cahill, page 25 top, page 191 bottom right

Scott Carpenter, page 39 bottom, page 47 bottom, page 177 bottom
Steven McGrath, page 29 center left, page 69 top
Stephanie Stragier, page 115 bottom right
Tara Lemezis, page 49 top
Tanner Martin, page 21 center, page 129 bottom right, page 156 top, page 171 bottom, page 187 bottom left
Vasura Jayaweera, page 40

Alan Schmierer, page 100, top left
Scott Heron, page 91 bottom

Judy Gallagher, page 76
Nigel Tate, page 61 center left

All illustrations by **Bologna Sandwich**

INDEX

C

D

O

P

T

TOM MYERS

An elementary school teacher and birder who lives in Oregon. He began birding in 2017 after he bought a kayak and started noticing birds while he paddled. Since then, he finds and photographs birds whenever possible. When he's not teaching or birding, Tom stays busy reading, beekeeping, and baking. His bird photography and links to his "Bird of the Week" videos can be found on his website, www.birdertom.com. His favorite bird is the Short-eared Owl.